"I cannot think of a subject more important to this generation than ethics or a person better to treat it than C. Ben Mitchell. I'm very happy to recommend this welcome and important volume."

Eric Metaxas, *New York Times* best-selling author, *Bonhoeffer: Pastor, Martyr, Prophet, Spy*

"In a world filled with test-tube babies, living wills, and drone warfare, Christian ethics can seem like quicksilver, with positions irrelevant almost as soon as they are articulated, due to fast-changing circumstances. This book demonstrates why and how every believer is called to Christ-conformed ethical reasoning. C. Ben Mitchell, one of the most significant Christian ethicists of our age, shares C. S. Lewis's gift for communicating complex issues in easily understood terms. This book brims with insight that transcends the ethical squabbles of any given moment. Most importantly, this book shows us how to be moral without surrendering to mere moralism by rooting and grounding our ethics in the gospel that saves."

Russell D. Moore, President, The Ethics and Religious Liberty Commission; author, *Tempted and Tried*

"C. Ben Mitchell has written what a volume appearing in a student's guide series should be. Both concise and precise, his guide to ethics and moral reasoning within the Christian tradition will give readers a sense of the questions they should explore and the resources to use in that exploration. For students whose cultural context leaves them adrift in a sea of conflicting moral claims, Mitchell is a seasoned, reliable navigator."

Gilbert Meilaender, Duesenberg Professor in Christian Ethics, Valparaiso University

"C. Ben Mitchell has written a concise, surefooted guide to ethics and moral reasoning from an evangelical perspective that takes both the Scriptures and the history of ethical discussion seriously. The text is written with admirable clarity and scholarly competence. For Mitchell, the triune God's divine design for human life is our flourishing as persons who are members of a moral community. This short book contributes to that flourishing, and I commend it enthusiastically."

Graham A. Cole, Anglican Professor of Divinity, Beeson Divinity School

"Every beginning student of ethics should rejoice at the publication of this book. Mitchell excels at describing our complicated ethical landscape without sacrificing depth or accuracy. I wish this introduction had been available when I was an undergraduate!"

Christina Bieber Lake, Clyde S. Kilby Professor of English, Wheaton College

ETHICS AND MORAL REASONING

RECLAIMING THE
CHRISTIAN INTELLECTUAL TRADITION

David S. Dockery, series editor

CONSULTING EDITORS

Hunter Baker
Timothy George
Niel Nielson
Philip G. Ryken
Michael J. Wilkins
John D. Woodbridge

OTHER RCIT VOLUMES:

The Great Tradition of Christian Thinking, David S. Dockery and
    Timothy George
The Liberal Arts, Gene C. Fant Jr.
Political Thought, Hunter Baker
Literature, Louis Markos
Philosophy, David K. Naugle
Christian Worldview, Philip G. Ryken

ETHICS AND MORAL REASONING
A STUDENT'S GUIDE

C. Ben Mitchell

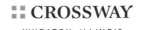

CROSSWAY
WHEATON, ILLINOIS

Trade paperback ISBN: 978-1-4335-3767-7
PDF ISBN: 978-1-4335-3768-4
Mobipocket ISBN: 978-1-4335-3769-1
ePub ISBN: 978-1-4335-3770-7

Library of Congress Catlaoging-in-Publication Data

Mitchell, C. Ben.
   Ethics and moral reasoning : a student's guide / C. Ben Mitchell, David S. Dockery, series editor.
      pages cm. -- (Reclaiming the Christian intellectual tradition)
   Includes bibliographical references and index.
   ISBN 978-1-4335-3767-7 (tp)
1. Christian ethics. I. Title.
BJ1151.M58 2013
241—dc23   2013023903

Crossway is a publishing ministry of Good News Publishers.

VP		23	22	21	20	19	18	17	16	15	14	13
15	14	13	12	11	10	9	8	7	6	5	4	3	2	1

To Nancy,
the wife of my youth and
the most ethical person I have ever known.

CONTENTS

SERIES PREFACE

RECLAIMING THE CHRISTIAN INTELLECTUAL TRADITION

The Reclaiming the Christian Intellectual Tradition series is designed to provide an overview of the distinctive way the church has read the Bible, formulated doctrine, provided education, and engaged the culture. The contributors to this series all agree that personal faith and genuine Christian piety are essential for the life of Christ followers and for the church. These contributors also believe that helping others recognize the importance of serious thinking about God, Scripture, and the world needs a renewed emphasis at this time in order that the truth claims of the Christian faith can be passed along from one generation to the next. The study guides in this series will enable us to see afresh how the Christian faith shapes how we live, how we think, how we write books, how we govern society, and how we relate to one another in our churches and social structures. The richness of the Christian intellectual tradition provides guidance for the complex challenges that believers face in this world.

This series is particularly designed for Christian students and others associated with college and university campuses, including faculty, staff, trustees, and other various constituents. The contributors to the series will explore how the Bible has been interpreted in the history of the church, as well as how theology has been formulated. They will ask: How does the Christian faith influence our understanding of culture, literature, philosophy, government, beauty, art, or work? How does the Christian intellectual tradition help us understand truth? How does the Christian intellectual tradition shape our approach to education? We believe that this series is not only timely but that it meets an important need, because the secular culture in which we now find ourselves is, at best, indifferent to the Christian faith, and the Christian world—at least in its more popular forms—tends to be confused about the beliefs, heritage, and tradition associated with the Christian faith.

At the heart of this work is the challenge to prepare a generation of Christians to think Christianly, to engage the academy and the culture, and to serve church and society. We believe that both the breadth and the depth of the Christian intellectual tradition need to be reclaimed, revitalized, renewed, and revived for us to carry forward this work. These study guides will seek to provide a framework to help introduce students to the great tradition of Christian thinking, seeking to highlight its importance for understanding the world, its significance for serving both church and society, and its application for Christian thinking and learning. The series is a starting point for exploring important ideas and issues such as truth, meaning, beauty, and justice.

We trust that the series will help introduce readers to the apostles, church fathers, Reformers, philosophers, theologians, historians, and a wide variety of other significant thinkers. In addition to well-known leaders such as Clement, Origen, Augustine, Thomas Aquinas, Martin Luther, and Jonathan Edwards, readers will be pointed to William Wilberforce, G. K. Chesterton, T. S. Eliot, Dorothy Sayers, C. S. Lewis, Johann Sebastian Bach, Isaac Newton, Johannes Kepler, George Washington Carver, Elizabeth Fox-Genovese, Michael Polanyi, Henry Luke Orombi, and many others. In doing so, we hope to introduce those who throughout history have demonstrated that it is indeed possible to be serious about the life of the mind while simultaneously being deeply committed Christians. These efforts to strengthen serious Christian thinking and scholarship will not be limited to the study of theology, scriptural interpretation, or philosophy, even though these areas provide the framework for understanding the Christian faith for all other areas of exploration. In order for us to reclaim and advance the Christian intellectual tradition, we must have some understanding of the tradition itself. The volumes in this series will seek to explore this tradition and its application for our twenty-first-century world. Each volume contains a glossary, study questions, and a list of resources for further study, which we trust will provide helpful guidance for our readers.

I am deeply grateful to the series editorial committee: Timothy George, John Woodbridge, Michael Wilkins, Niel Nielson, Philip Ryken, and Hunter Baker. Each of these colleagues joins me in thanking our various contributors for their fine work. We all express our appreciation to Justin Taylor, Jill Carter, Allan Fisher, Lane Dennis, and the Crossway team for their enthusiastic support for the project. We offer the project with the hope that students will be helped, faculty and Christian leaders will be encouraged, institutions will be strengthened, churches will be built up, and, ultimately, that God will be glorified.

Soli Deo Gloria
David S. Dockery
Series Editor

AUTHOR'S PREFACE

Few people need to be convinced of the importance of ethics. We live in a tragically flawed world where we are confronted daily with moral failures. People lie, commit adultery, steal from their employers, and pollute the environment. At the same time, we all know people whose lives reflect personal integrity, sacrificial love, and unimpeachable virtue. We know that ethics is important at all levels of society. Whether presidents or members of Congress, CEOs or their employees, doctors or nurses, teachers or pupils, or parents or children, we all believe it is important to make good moral decisions, to be ethical people.

What might take some convincing is the notion that we could ever come to common conclusions about ethics. There is deep skepticism in our culture about moral agreement. In his study of the religious and spiritual lives of emerging adults ages eighteen to twenty-three years old, Notre Dame sociologist Christian Smith found that

> emerging adults have been raised in a world involving certain outlooks and assumptions that they have clearly absorbed and that they in turn largely affirm and reinforce. Stated in philosophical terms, their world has undergone a significant epistemic and axiological breakdown. It is difficult if not impossible in this world that has come to be to actually know anything objectively real or true that can be rationally maintained in a way that might require people actually to change their minds or lives. Emerging adults know quite well how they personally were raised in their families, and they know fairly well how they generally "feel" about things. But they are also aware that all knowledge and value are historically conditioned and culturally relative. And

they have not, in our view, been equipped with the intellectual and moral tools to know what to do with that fact. So most simply choose to believe and live by whatever subjectively feels "right" to them, and to try not to seriously assess, much less criticize, anything else that anyone else has chosen to believe, feel, or do. Whether or not they use these words to say it, for most emerging adults, in the end, it's all relative. One thought or opinion isn't more defensible than any other. One way of life cannot claim to be better than others. Some moral beliefs may personally *feel* right, but no moral belief can rationally claim to be really true, because that implies criticizing or discounting other moral beliefs. And that would be rude, presumptuous, intolerant, and unfeeling. This is what we mean when we use the terms *crisis* and *breakdown*. . . .

Many know there must be something more, and they want it. Many are uncomfortable with their inability to make trust statements and moral claims without killing them with the death of a thousand qualifications. But they do not know what to do about that, given the crisis of truth and values that has destabilized their culture. And so they simply carry on as best they can, as sovereign, autonomous, empowered individuals who lack a reliable basis for any particular conviction or direction by which to guide their lives.[1]

This state of affairs sounds dire because it is. This is the world many of my students inhabit. And, in most cases, it's not their fault. They have inherited this worldview from social media, schoolmates, pop culture, and sometimes even from their parents. They intuit that this is not the way it's supposed to be, but it's the only way they know. When they look to my own Boomer generation, they do not see many attractive alternatives.

Because the culture is largely relativistic, we also often trade ethics for legal compliance. If someone asks, "Is it ethical to do X?," it is likely that someone will respond, "The policy [or the law] says do X." Ethical right and wrong are confused with legal right

---

[1] Christian Smith with Patricia Snell, *Souls in Transition: The Religious and Spiritual Lives of Emerging Adults* (New York: Oxford University Press, 2009), 292–93, 294.

and wrong. But to comply with law and/or policy is not necessarily to act ethically. The law or policy could be wrong. Just because what Hitler did was legal in Nazi Germany does not mean it was right. Just because chattel slavery was legal in the South in the 1860s did not make it right to own slaves. Sometimes it is right to disobey the law. Sometimes we are morally obligated to quit a job or blow the whistle over immoral policies.

These are some of the issues we will explore in this volume. The terrain is not always easy to traverse, but perseverance has its rewards. As a great Catholic thinker, A. G. Sertillanges, once said, "Truth serves only its slaves."[2]

THE LANGUAGE OF ETHICS

Before we go further, I should point out that like every other discipline, ethics and moral reasoning have their own language. Ethics and moral reasoning fit in the category called "axiology." The big three questions of philosophy include metaphysics (What is?), epistemology (How do you know?), and axiology (What is value? and What is valuable?).

Axiological questions may apply to economics if we ask how we determine value monetarily. Axiology may also apply to art if we explore aesthetic value. Axiology applies to ethics when we think about moral value. So if metaphysics asks, "What is truth?," axiology asks, "What is beauty?" and "What is good?" The true, the good, and the beautiful are important subjects indeed.

This book is a guide to thinking about the good. We can think about the good in several ways. First, we may *describe* good behavior, decisions, or attitudes. Descriptive ethics attempts merely to describe a certain moral state of affairs. For instance, "Dr. Jack Kevorkian ended the life of at least 130 patients through physician-assisted suicide and euthanasia." This statement merely de-

[2] A. G. Sertillanges, *The Intellectual Life: Its Spirit, Conditions, Methods* (1934; repr. Washington, DC: Catholic University of America Press, 1987), 4.

scribes Dr. Kevorkian's behavior without making a judgment about whether it was good or bad, right or wrong.

Prescriptive or normative ethics takes us into the realm of words such as *right, wrong, good, bad, ought, ought not, should, should not, obligated,* and *nonobligated.* This is the language of moral assessment. If I say, "Dr. Jack Kevorkian should not have ended the life of his patients," I am rendering a moral judgment about his behavior. I am saying he was wrong to do so. I am *pre-scribing* what his moral behavior *should* have been and implying that it should be normative for other physicians, too.

Applied ethics is simply bringing the tools of prescriptive ethics to bear on issues or disciplines such that we talk about the ethics of abortion, capital punishment, war, the environment, or genetic engineering. Similarly, we can *apply* normative concepts to a variety of disciplines and discuss business ethics, medical ethics, legal ethics, nursing ethics, pharmacy ethics, military ethics, and so on.

Lastly, metaethics considers what we mean when we use words such as *good.* How do we define the word *good?*

In sum, every area of ethics is ultimately concerned with moral goodness as a way of determining right conduct, attitudes, and character.

Because I am a Christian, I am concerned about how conduct, attitudes, and character should be oriented toward the triune God through Jesus Christ by the power of the indwelling Spirit. At the same time I must ask myself, in light of that relationship, how I am to behave toward others. These three moral relationships—to God, to others, and to self—define the ethical territory.

This is exactly how the ancient Jews and Christians understood their ethical duties. When a lawyer came to Jesus and asked him which commandment was the most important, Jesus replied:

> The most important is, "Hear, O Israel: The Lord our God, the Lord is one. And you shall love the Lord your God with all your heart and with all your soul and with all your mind and with all

your strength." The second is this: "You shall love your neighbor as yourself." There is no other commandment greater than these. (Mark 12:29–31)

Jesus described a trinity of moral relationships—to God, to others, and to self. These three relationships were to be ordered by the virtue of love. Importantly, when one of these relationships becomes disordered, the others are affected. If one's relationship with God is broken or distorted, one's relationship with others will be negatively impacted, and one's relationship with oneself will also be affected. Similarly, if one's relationship with others is disordered, one's relationship with God and self will be negatively impacted. Jesus alluded to this reality in the Sermon on the Mount when he taught about anger:

> So if you are offering your gift at the altar and there remember that your brother has something against you, leave your gift there before the altar and go. First be reconciled to your brother, and then come and offer your gift. (Matt. 5:23–24)

Before God can be worshiped rightly, our strained relationships with others must be made right. Once our relationship with our brother or sister is reordered and reconciliation takes place, our relationship with God is reordered so that worship is unhindered. Rightly ordered loves not only mark the moral life of the faithful believer but also are the means of human flourishing, of having a right relationship with the God who is the personification of the true, the good, and the beautiful.

ACKNOWLEDGMENTS

I begin this book by thanking the series editors for the kind invitation to offer a volume on ethics and moral reasoning. I first met David Dockery in 1980 when we were in seminary together. From the beginning of our relationship I was struck by his personal character. Even as a student, he was a man of deep Christian commitment, profound integrity, careful scholarship, and immense practical wisdom. David has been a trusted advisor and friend since those seminary days. More than once we just missed working together. He hired me to teach ethics at The Southern Baptist Theological Seminary but left to become president at Union University before I could get to Louisville. Another opportunity to work on the same faculty almost came to fruition but was not meant to be. The opportunity to partner with David Dockery is one reason it is such an honor and privilege for me to be teaching at Union University now.

I first met Timothy George just after seminary, when he was still a relatively new professor at Southern Seminary. After meeting him the first time, I was certain I wanted to pursue doctoral work in historical theology under his tutelage. His knowledge of Christian theology is so vast, his personality so irenic, and his churchmanship so evident. Alas, he embarked on a year-long sabbatical, and I ended up leaving Louisville before he returned. Nevertheless, we too have been friends since then, and I am grateful to have been able to teach an ethics course several times at Beeson Divinity School.

So it is especially gratifying to be able to join these mentors, colleagues, and friends in the Recovering the Christian Intellectual Tradition series.

Friendship has been an important theme from Aristotle to C. S. Lewis. I would be remiss if I did not also acknowledge the formative influence of several special friends. I came to faith in Christ under the ministry of Robert L. Mounts. An amazing Bible teacher, Bob has been a confidant, mentor, and friend for nearly forty years. Among many other things, I owe to Bob the observation about the trinity of relationships that is part of the author's preface.

Paul House, Greg Thornbury, and Richard Bailey have also been friends for many years. We share many great memories of our time together at Southern Seminary, of trips to see Carl F. H. Henry, and of annual family gatherings at Thanksgiving. We have wept a bit with one another and laughed a lot.

Finally, one of the most delightful things about being at Union University is the fantastic colleagues with whom I am privileged to serve. In addition to the finest administration I have ever seen, the School of Theology and Missions is a wonderful context in which to work. By their example, my colleagues inspire me to be a better professor. Thursday tea time with them has become a highlight of my week. Also, almost since the day I arrived at Union, I have been meeting every Friday with a marvelous group of faculty colleagues across a number of disciplines to discuss everything under the sun. And sometimes we even talk about the sun. They have become an indispensable part of my life both academically and personally. I owe a great debt to them for their passion for truth, keen insights, and Christlike charity.

For nearly a decade I had the wonderful experience of not only teaching with Graham Cole at Trinity Evangelical Divinity School but also being next-door neighbors with him and his wife, Julie. Graham may have saved my life by reminding me that "we are creatures before we are Christians" and that living life to its fullest is not necessarily the same as going as fast as one can—a lesson I'm still trying to apply.

✚ 1

THE CHALLENGES OF A RELATIVIST WORLD

"Well, that might be right for you, but not for me."

"You can't judge one culture by another."

"Who's to say what's right or wrong?"

Most of us have heard comments like those while talking with someone over coffee or at a dinner party. The idea that morality is personal, subjective, and relative is in the air we breathe. It's part of the Zeitgeist (the spirit of the times). In a widely used introductory ethics text, J. L. Mackie confidently exclaimed, "There are no objective values."[1] Notably, the subtitle of Mackie's volume is "Inventing Right and Wrong." According to Mackie, moral values are human inventions. This is a remarkable claim indeed, but one that seems a commonplace today.

Similarly, in her often reprinted essay "In Defense of Moral Relativism," American anthropologist Ruth Benedict wrote,

> We recognize that morality differs in every society, and it is a convenient term for socially approved habits. Mankind has always preferred to say, "It is morally good," rather than "It is habitual," and the fact of this preference is enough for a critical science of ethics. But historically the two phrases are synonymous.[2]

---

[1] J. L. Mackie, *Ethics: Inventing Right from Wrong* (New York: Penguin, 1977).

[2] Ruth Benedict, "A Defense of Ethical Relativism," in *Knowledge, Nature, and Norms: An Introduction to Philosophy*, ed. Mark Timmons and David Shoemaker (New York: Wadsworth Cengage Learning, 2008), 329.

For Benedict, ethical behavior is just the habits we call "good." There are no objective, universal ethical norms; there are only the habits we call our ethics. Those habits are relative; they differ in every society.

Benedict was right about one thing—we live in a morally relativistic world. What does that mean? First, it means that if relativism is true, then the study of ethics and moral reasoning is merely a quaint search for dusty, old ideas that no one really believes any longer, a little like hunting for antiques. If relativism is true, it also means that the search for enduring, universal moral norms is futile. But the fact that we live in a relativistic world also means that if relativism is *not* true, we need to know how to respond to a view that is so pervasive in our culture. And it is not only pervasive; relativism is morally crippling because it relegates ethical discussions to the personal, private, and subjective, and to the realm of mere preference.

What we need to realize is that relativism is not merely an assertion. Oh, some people do assert it, but it is in fact an argument for a particular way of understanding morality. Only by understanding the argument will we be better prepared to respond to the claims relativists make.

The argument for what we might call "normative ethical relativism" has two premises and a conclusion. It is "normative" in that it maintains it is the way things *should* be. It is relativistic because it claims that notions of right and wrong or good and bad should *not* be the same for everyone, everywhere, at all times.

Louis Pojman, the late philosopher who taught for many years at the United States Military Academy, calls the two premises of normative ethical relativism the diversity thesis and the dependency thesis.

THE DIVERSITY THESIS

The diversity thesis is that notions of right and wrong differ from person to person and culture to culture. This premise of the argument seems patently true if we understand it merely as a description of the diversity of cultural norms and mores. For instance, in most Arabic cultures, displaying the bottom of the foot is disrespectful. In some African cultures, giving a gift with the left hand is an insult. Neither of those practices is insulting in American culture. So it is true that ideas about what is right or wrong differ from one culture to another and sometimes from one person or family to another. As Benedict said, "We recognize that morality differs in every society." But that is merely a description of the way things are. This premise does not by itself make the moral claim that that is the way it *ought* to be.

THE DEPENDENCY THESIS

The second premise of the argument for normative ethical relativism is the dependency thesis, which holds that morality depends on human nature, the human condition, or specific sociocultural circumstances, or a combination of all three.

The word *depends* here implies that one's views of right and wrong rest solely on one or more of the contingencies just mentioned. So the claim is, first, that what is right or wrong might depend upon human nature. For instance, some people believe that right and wrong are determined by the ability of human beings and other animals to experience conscious pleasure or pain. This view is known as "ethical hedonism." The ethical hedonist believes that it is always wrong to cause pain and always right to cause pleasure or at least to minimize pain. One person who holds this view is Peter Singer, an Australian philosopher who teaches at Princeton University. Because Singer holds that it is wrong to do anything that causes pain to conscious beings, he has become an outspoken opponent of capital punishment and outspoken proponent of vegetarianism. Not only is it always wrong, he argues, to cause pain to other human beings, but because he considers animals to be conscious beings, it is also wrong to cause unnecessary pain to other animals. Because humans do not need to eat animals to survive, causing pain by killing them for food or clothing is immoral. Hence, what is right or wrong for Singer depends on the ability for a creature to experience pleasure or pain.

A relativist might also maintain that what's right and wrong depends upon the human condition, such as that humans are mortal. Much of our behavior as a species does seem to be aimed at survival. Our mortality—the fact that we can and do die—leads us to avoid certain behaviors and even to ban those behaviors by law. If human beings were like some of the characters, say, in Arnold Schwarzenegger's *Terminator* movies, we might not have laws against certain forms of physical harm. What would be the harm, for instance, in blasting off someone's arm with a weapon if the arm would regenerate in a matter of seconds? Or what would be the harm in killing people if they could somehow recombine or reconstitute? Because humans are mortal, we tend to be more or less risk averse. Morality, the relativist might say, is just a response to our risk-averse tendencies.

Or, perhaps, our moral notions are the result of our familial or social upbringing. Maybe our society dictates what we think is right and wrong. We sometimes call this view "cultural relativism," but it is a species of the same argument that we have been discussing. Since each culture has its own moral code, the most we can claim, says the relativist, is that morality depends upon one's social conditioning. As Benedict claimed, "It is habitual," and that is identical to saying, "It is morally good."

Finally, an ethical relativist might want to argue that our morality—our notions of right and wrong or good and bad—depends on some combination of all three inputs: human nature, the human condition, *and* human culture. Since every culture has its own views of what constitutes right or wrong conduct, since every culture has its own expression of risk aversion, and since every culture has its own social standards and practices, the following conclusion is warranted, says the relativist: Morality—notions of right and wrong, good and bad, obligation and non-obligation—*should* differ from culture to culture. Note the inclusion of the word that implies moral obligation: *should*. This is the way that it should be. It should be the case that morality differs from person to person and culture to culture. The normative ethical relativist claims that ethical pluralism is the best we can achieve, so that the notion that one's ethical views could be right—everywhere, for everyone, at all times—is mistaken at best and fascist at worst. Moreover, to critique another person's or culture's morality is a lack of hospitality at best and a moral assault at worst.

This is the moral world in which we live today. Sociologist Christian Smith, director of the study of religion and society at Notre Dame University, has spent much of his career analyzing the spiritual lives of teenagers and emerging adults. In his 2011 study, *Lost in Transition: The Dark Side of Emerging Adulthood*, Professor Smith found that 30 percent of the emerging adults he interviewed professed a belief in strong moral relativism, compared with a national survey showing as many as 47 percent of American emerging adults agreeing with this statement: "Morals are relative, there are not definite rights and wrongs for everybody."[3]

How do we respond to normative ethical relativism? Well, not with a mere assertion. That is, we should not respond by saying only, "No, that's wrong." That would be to respond to an argument with an assertion. Because relativism is an argument, a counter argument is needed. To construct a counter argument, one must either respond to the premises or show that the argument is invalid, or both.

Normative ethical relativism faces some significant challenges. One classic response to normative ethical relativism was offered by John Hospers, who was for many years chair of the department

---

[3] Christian Smith, Kari Christoffersen, Hilary Davidson, and Patricia Snell Herzog, *Lost in Transition: The Dark Side of Emerging Adulthood* (New York: Oxford, 2011), 27.

of philosophy at the University of Southern California.[4] Hospers suggested that one problem with relativism is its claim that what is right in one group is wrong in another. As it turns out, observed Hospers, we are part of multiple groups. For instance, we share membership in the species *Homo sapiens*; we also are members of families, churches, geographical communities, interest groups (clubs and athletic teams), etc. Which groups form our moral community, the community that shapes our ethics? Why that group and not another? And just because the majority of any particular group thinks something is right does not make it right. It would be very easy to say, "Cannibalism is right in a cannibalistic culture, and if most of the people in the United States became cannibals, then cannibalism would be right for us." But is there any reason to believe that just because the majority practices cannibalism, it is therefore right? Is the habit of cannibalism the same as approving an ethic of cannibalism? Majorities can be—and historically have been—wrong. Is the relativist really prepared to argue that if a majority of Americans approved of slavery, slavery would be right?

Another problem with the relativist argument is that moral error is not possible if relativism is true. The relativist, at least a consistent one, cannot say that someone made an ethical mistake. The relativist could break a law, commit a mistake of etiquette, or violate community standards, but she could not commit a moral wrong, since right and wrong are in the eyes of the beholder. Is it really possible that having sex with a child is only a violation of community standards? It seems perfectly reasonable, indeed necessary, to say that child sexual abuse is a moral wrong, everywhere and at all times.

A third problem is that there is no place for moral reformers in relativism. If a community holds that apartheid is morally right, then according to the relativist argument, who is Nelson Mandela

---

[4] John Hospers, *Human Conduct: An Introduction to the Problem of Ethics* (New York: Harcourt, 1961), 37–39.

to claim that racial segregation is wrong? If relativism is true, Abraham Lincoln was wrong to challenge American chattel slavery, and the Reverend Martin Luther King Jr. was wrong to call for an end to racial discrimination.

Fourth, relativism suffers from a fundamental philosophical problem. Remember that the relativist argument begins with a descriptive premise claiming that morality differs from person to person and culture to culture. The argument then claims that this is the way it *ought* to be. An "ought" claim cannot be derived from an "is" claim. In other words, just because this is the way things are does not mean this is the way things ought to be. Just because some Brahmans in India practiced suttee—the ritual practice of burning widows to death—does not mean that is how the culture ought to function. Just because some Islamist and African cultures practice female genital mutilation does not thereby make the practice correct or morally defensible.

Finally, relativism fails to distinguish between moral practices and the values that underwrite them. For instance, in one culture, exposing the bottom of one's feet may well be a serious moral insult. In another culture, it may be considered wrong to make a certain hand gesture while driving if someone cuts you off at an intersection. What both cultures seem to value in calling those behaviors wrong is *respect for others*. It is out of respect for others that one avoids showing the bottom of one's feet in Arab cultures, and it is out of respect for others that one avoids certain hand gestures while driving. Every culture seems to value respect, even though the reasons for doing so or the persons seen to be deserving of respect may differ.

Likewise, while living on the North Shore of Chicago, I observed that public relations entrepreneurs in that community thought it was proper to retaliate legally if someone stole their brand name or brand logo. At the same time, gang members in the inner city thought it was proper to retaliate violently if a rival gang killed one of their gang members. In both cases, the underlying value that dictated behavior was a form of justice or fairness. The grounds and objects of justice were different, to be sure, but some notion of fairness informed the attitude and behavior of both the Windy City entrepreneur and the gang member.

In his interesting volume *The Moral Sense*, political scientist James Q. Wilson argued that every culture shares the values of sympathy, fairness, self-control, and duty, among others.[5] These values reflect the moral intuitions of a common humanity. So, although on the surface moral practices and beliefs may indeed differ, in fact, human beings share an amazingly robust set of ethical ideals across cultures. Therefore, relativism is wrong. The moral sense—those foundational values—does not differ from person to person and culture to culture. Though none of these critiques alone may convince a person that relativism's foundation is suspect, together they provide substantial evidence that relativism is unsound.[6] "Most of us have a moral sense," Wilson maintained, "but some of us have tried to talk ourselves out of it. It is as if a person born to appreciate a golden sunset or lovely song had persuaded himself and others that a greasy smear or clanging gong ought to be enjoyed as much as true beauty."[7]

Although relativism is unjustifiable morally, that does not answer the questions, What's right, what's wrong, and how do you know? Those questions take us back to the beginning.

---

[5] James Q. Wilson, *The Moral Sense* (New York: Free Press, 1997).

[6] For additional critiques of relativism see Francis A. Beckwith, *Relativism: Feet Firmly Planted in Mid-Air* (Grand Rapids, MI: Baker, 1998); Peter Kreeft, *A Refutation of Moral Relativism: Interviews with an Absolutist* (San Francisco: Ignatius Press, 1999); and Timothy Mosteller, *Relativism: A Guide for the Perplexed* (New York: Continuum, 2008).

[7] Wilson, *The Moral Sense*, ix.

✚ 2

THE HISTORY OF MORAL REASONING, PART 1

Western civilization is indebted to the Judeo-Christian tradition for its notions of human dignity and human rights, its innovation in science and medicine, its habits of humanitarian charity and universal education, and its rich contribution to the arts. "Religion has written much of the history of the West," observes Jewish scholar Jacob Neusner.[1] Roger Scruton, the British polymath, has put it this way:

> Throughout its most flourishing periods, Western civilization has produced a culture which happily absorbs and adapts the cultures of other places, other faiths, and other times. Its basic fund of stories, its moral precepts, and its religious imagery come from the Hebrew Bible and the Greek New Testament.[2]

Even the notorious atheist Christopher Hitchens agreed that Western culture makes little sense without attending to the contribution of biblical religion: "You are not educated," he maintained, "if you don't know the Bible. You can't read Shakespeare or Milton without it."[3] So it is right and good to begin at the beginning with the Old Testament.

---

[1] Jacob Neusner, ed., *Religious Foundations of Western Civilization: Judaism, Christianity, and Islam* (Nashville: Abingdon, 2006), *xi*.
[2] Roger Scruton, *Culture Counts: Faith and Feeling in a World Besieged* (New York: Encounter Books, 2007), 3.
[3] Quoted in Mindy Belz, "The World According to Hitch," *WORLD* magazine, June 2, 2006, http://www.worldmag.com/articles/11908 (accessed March 20, 2008).

OLD TESTAMENT ETHICS

We are barely into the biblical text before the vocabulary of value is used:

> And God said, "Let there be light," and there was light. And God saw that the light was *good*. And God separated the light from the darkness. (Gen. 1:3–4)

The refrain "God saw that it was good" is repeated in verses 10, 12, 18, 21, and 25, and in verse 31 we read, "God saw everything that he had made, and behold, it was *very good*." The meaning of the Hebrew word for good (*tobh*) is quite fluid in the Old Testament. According to Old Testament professor Kenneth Matthews the word can mean "happy, beneficial, aesthetically beautiful, morally righteous, preferable, of superior quality, or of ultimate value."[4]

Notice the chain of divine agency: the holy God said, "Let there be . . ." And it was so. And it was good. "Good" in this case seems to point to conformity to the will and purpose of God, in whom we see the true, the good, and the beautiful. "It is good" was not a statement made relative to any other created thing. God's only comparison was with his own purpose and will. God is good, and all that he made is good.

MARRIAGE AND FAMILY

God said it was very good that he made humanity, male and female, in his own image and likeness, to multiply and steward the earth and its plants and animals. From the beginning, humans were created to procreate. And we are told in Genesis 2:23–24 that they were to exercise their procreative gifts in the context of a "one flesh" kind of relationship—marriage. One-flesh unity includes the sexual, procreative aspect and much more. Through married procreation, offspring are born as a token of God's blessing. So the

---

[4] Kenneth A. Matthews, *Genesis 1–11:26*, New American Commentary (Nashville: Broadman, 1996), 146.

psalmist declared, "Behold, children are a heritage from the LORD, the fruit of the womb a reward" (Ps. 127:3).

The Genesis texts are the origin of a tradition that has served humanity well for millennia. Indeed, it was not until the mid-twentieth century that the following axioms came under serious challenge:

- One should refrain from sexual activity until marriage (i.e., the wedding).
- An essential and normative (though not the only) purpose of marriage is to produce children.
- One should choose a spouse from the opposite sex.
- One should refrain from sexual activity with anyone but one's spouse.
- The marital estate is intended to be a permanent relationship of covenantal love until death.

Because of a half-century of assault, many people think these maxims seem quaint, if not completely antiquated. Make no mistake about it, however; these have been among the great pillars of Western civilization. Their rejection will result not only in personal trauma but in cultural chaos. Cohabitation, adultery, divorce, and same-sex relationships wreak havoc in people's lives and slowly erode the ballast that keeps the culture stable.

LABOR AND VOCATION

Innovation and development have been other trademarks of the West. Rooted in the mandate to "be fertile and increase, fill the earth and master it; and rule the fish of the sea, the birds of the sky, and all the living things that creep on earth" (Gen. 1:28 NJPS), the Judeo-Christian tradition provides rich impetus for the stewardship of invention.

God put primordial humans in a garden "to till it and tend it" (Gen. 2:15 NJPS), to classify the natural order (Gen. 2:20), and to sustain them and the garden. It is important to notice that the dignity of work was evident before the curse was pronounced on human rebellion. It was not until after the fall that labor became toilsome and bread had to be earned by the sweat of the brow (Gen. 3:17).

The first humans made tools (Gen. 4:22), planted vineyards (Gen. 9:20), made weapons (Gen. 10:9), and built great cities (Gen. 10:10). *Homo sapiens* (human knowers) were by their very nature *Homo faber* (human fabricators). Inventiveness and innovation were characteristics of the ancients, as it is today.

Among Jews and Christians, honest labor has been an important validation of human dignity. Jewish philosopher Moses Maimonides (1135–1204) honored both work and the worker when he said, "Just as the employer is warned not to steal the wages of the poor and not to delay them, so is the poor person warned not to steal the work of the employer by idling a little here and a little there, until he passes the whole day in deceit. Rather, he must be scrupulous with himself regarding time."[5] Likewise early Christians valued work highly. Jesus, after all, grew up in a carpenter's home, most of the disciples were bi-vocational, and the apostle Paul admonished Christians to avoid "any brother who is walking in idleness and not in accord with the tradition that you received from us. . . . If anyone is not willing to work, let him not eat" (2 Thess. 3:6, 10). Paul also enjoined the faithful "to do their work quietly and to earn their own living" (2 Thess. 3:12).

Against the medieval tendency to dichotomize work as either sacred or secular, the Reformers saw all work as sacred vocation (*vocatio*). Martin Luther famously argued that all (morally virtuous) work is God's work and is to be done so as to glorify God and serve others. This was the origin of the so-called Protestant work ethic that was analyzed and critiqued by Max Weber in *The Protestant Ethic and the Spirit of Capitalism* (first English translation in 1930).

---

[5] Moses Maimonides, *A Maimonides Reader*, ed. Isadore Twersky (Springfield, NJ: Behrman, 1972), 182.

SANCTITY AND DIGNITY OF HUMAN LIFE

Another hallmark of the West emerging from the Genesis account is the sanctity of every human life. According to the Hebrew Bible, all human beings owe their ancestry to a set of common parents, Adam and Eve, who were made in the image and likeness of their creator (Gen. 1:27). All their progeny bear the *imago Dei* (image of God) as well (Gen. 5:1–32). From these beginnings we have inherited the concept of human exceptionalism—the affirmation that human beings are unique among the created order and possessors of inalienable rights and ought to exercise managerial stewardship over nature. The doctrine of the sanctity of human life brought with it a number of significant implications. Infanticide, abortion, and brutality were rejected as inconsistent with the doctrine of the *imago Dei*. Moreover, belief in human dignity became the foundation of gender and racial equality in the West.

INFANTICIDE AND ABORTION

European historian W. E. H. Lecky called infanticide "one of the deepest stains of the ancient civilisation." Judaism consistently prohibited it because the practice violated the image of God. The first-century Jewish historian Josephus wrote, "The law orders all the offspring to be brought up, and forbids women either to cause abortion or to make away with the fetus." The Hebrew origins of the sanctity of human life provided the moral framework for early Christian condemnation of infanticide against the bleak backdrop of the barbarism of Roman culture. For instance, an early Christian handbook, the *Didache* (c. 85–110), sometimes called "The Teachings of the Twelve Apostles," commanded: "Thou shalt not murder a child by abortion nor kill them when born."

Some biblical scholars have argued that the New Testament's silence on abortion per se is due to the fact that it was simply beyond the pale of early Christian practice. Because of Christians' affirmation of Hebrew understandings of the sanctity of human life, they could not countenance abortion. But they did not just condemn abortion and infanticide; Christian communities were at the forefront of providing alternatives, including adopting children who were destined to be abandoned by their parents. Callistus (died c. 223) provided refuge to abandoned children by placing them in Christian homes. Benignus of Dijon (third century) offered nourishment and protection to abandoned children, including some with disabilities caused by failed abortions.

GLADIATORIAL BRUTALITY

In addition to repudiating infanticide, child abandonment, and abortion, Jews and early Christians denounced human sacrifices, suicide, and the gladiatorial games. Because of their conviction of the special dignity of every human being, they found the games detestable. Since the gladiators were usually criminals, prisoners of war, or slaves, in the eyes of the Romans their lives were expendable. But in the eyes of church leaders the practice was barbaric, and they called on Christians to boycott the "games."

GENDER EQUALITY

In both Judaism and Christianity, women and men are viewed as equal in nature—both being made in the image and likeness of God. Hence, in biblical times women held positions of high honor. The Ten Commandments require obedience to both father and mother. Deborah, a prophetess, was a judge in Israel; and seven of the fifty-five biblical prophets were women, according to Jewish teaching.

Among the Greeks, however, women were treated very differently. For instance, Homer had his character Agamemnon exclaim, "One cannot trust women." This terrible attitude toward women meant that female infanticide was morally permissible in Greece, since having a son was much more desirable than having a daughter. And Roman women were treated no better.

In contrast, the New Testament Gospels show Jesus of Nazareth treating women with great respect. He broke the tradition of some of the rabbis, speaking with and listening to the Samaritan woman (John 4:5–29). He violated contemporary customs by teaching Mary and Martha (Luke 10:38–42; John 11:25–26). Christians of the apostolic age welcomed women, giving the status of "brother" to men and "sister" to women. Examples can be multiplied, but perhaps the greatest affirmation of the equal value of men and women is Paul's declaration in Galatians 3:28–29: "There is neither Jew nor Greek, there is neither slave nor free, there is neither male nor female, for you are all one in Christ Jesus. And if you are Christ's, then you are Abraham's offspring, heirs according to promise."

Based on this understanding, Western cultures have repudiated the Hindu practice of suttee, the Chinese practice of foot-binding, the African practice of female genital mutilation, and the Muslim devaluation of a woman's testimony in court. These practices are morally objectionable because they violate the dignity of women, who are made in God's image just as are men.

RACIAL EQUALITY

Human dignity also has implications for racial equality. In a culture in which slavery was normative, Paul's instruction to Philemon not to treat Onesimus as his slave, but as his brother, was revolutionary (Philem. 16). According to Lecky, Christians often freed slaves: "St. Melania was said to have emancipated 8,000 slaves; St. Ovidius, a rich martyr of Gaul, 5,000; Chromatius, a Roman prefect under Diocletian, 1,400; Hermes, a prefect in the reign of Trajan, 1,250."

A virulent form of slavery was revived in the seventeenth century in England and the eighteenth century in America. Long political and armed battles were fought to abolish the practice. One of the most noteworthy examples of the efforts to end the slave trade was that of William Wilberforce and his Clapham Group, whose motivation to abolish slavery was underwritten by belief in the special dignity of every human being. Artisan Josiah Wedgewood even crafted a lapel pin to be worn by the abolitionists. The brooch showed an African slave, his shackled wrists lifted high, exclaiming, "Am I not a man and a brother?" This powerful image invoked the doctrine of human equality. And, although it took a civil war to end slavery in the United States, abolition was a product of the doctrine of human equality, which owes its origins to the God who inspired Genesis.

THE TEN COMMANDMENTS

"It is difficult to exaggerate the importance and significance of the Ten Commandments for Old Testament ethics," asserts Old Testament scholar and Christian educator Walter Kaiser. The same is true for the influence of the Ten Commandments on Western culture. In his magisterial *Law and Revolution: The Formation of the Western Legal Tradition*, distinguished Harvard jurist Harold J. Berman argued, "It is impossible to understand the revolutionary quality of the Western legal tradition without exploring its religious dimension,"[6] much of which is rooted in the Ten Commandments.

CHARACTERISTICS OF THE LAW

In order properly to understand Old Testament law, it is important to understand some of its general features. First, the law establishes broad principles and is not meant to cover every possible eventuality. The Ten Commandments, for instance, provide the substantive premises upon which Western law is built. The eighth commandment, "You shall not steal," has both negative and positive implications. Negatively, of course, the commandment forbids taking another person's property, but, positively, the command establishes

---

[6] Harold J. Berman, *Law and Revolution: The Formation of the Western Legal Tradition* (Cambridge, MA: Harvard University Press, 1983), 165.

the notion of owning private property. One cannot steal that which does not belong properly to another.

Second, the legal principles enshrined in the Ten Commandments have their origin in God himself. Since it is God who "spoke all these words" (Ex. 20:1), the law is not an invention of human ingenuity but a revelation of divine wisdom. Contrary to Thomas Hobbes's view in *Leviathan* that the origin of the law is the state, the state owes both its own origin and the law's origin to God.

Third, since God is the ultimate source of just laws, any offense against those laws is also an offense against God himself. So in King David's famous psalm of repentance he cries, "Against you, you only, have I sinned and done what is evil in your sight" (Ps. 51:4). Of course David knew that he had sinned against Bathsheba and her husband, Uriah, by committing adultery with her and having Uriah killed on the battlefield, but in his prayer David acknowledges that he lived *coram Deo* (before the face of God) and that his offense was ultimately an offense against the holy and loving law giver.

Finally, it is important to underscore the fact that biblical law forms the basis of Western jurisprudence. To take the commandment against stealing as an example again, Exodus 20:15 states the legal principle, "You shall not steal." In Deuteronomy 25:4, we have an illustration of the principle in the form of what we might call "case law": "You shall not muzzle an ox when it is treading out the grain." To do so would be a form of stealing that which, according to God and every wise farmer, properly belongs to the ox. In 1 Corinthians 9:9, 10, and 14, we have an application of the principle of the law in the New Testament. Paul defends his support for the ministry of the gospel. He makes his claim by appealing to the principles of the law:

> Do we not have the right to eat and drink? Do we not have the right to take along a believing wife, as do the other apostles and the brothers of the Lord and Cephas? Or is it only Barnabas and I who have no right to refrain from working for a living? Who serves as a soldier at his own expense? Who plants a vineyard

without eating any of its fruit? Or who tends a flock without getting some of the milk?

Do I say these things on human authority? Does not the Law say the same? For it is written in the Law of Moses, "You shall not muzzle an ox when it treads out the grain." Is it for oxen that God is concerned? Does he not certainly speak for our sake? It was written for our sake, because the plowman should plow in hope and the thresher thresh in hope of sharing in the crop. If we have sown spiritual things among you, is it too much if we reap material things from you? If others share this rightful claim on you, do not we even more?

Nevertheless, we have not made use of this right, but we endure anything rather than put an obstacle in the way of the gospel of Christ. Do you not know that those who are employed in the temple service get their food from the temple, and those who serve at the altar share in the sacrificial offerings? In the same way, the Lord commanded that those who proclaim the gospel should get their living by the gospel. (1 Cor. 9:4–14)

THE FIRST FOUR COMMANDMENTS

The first four commandments focus on the nature and worship of the law giver, while the last six commandments declare Israel's moral obligations to others. This is consistent with everything both Old and New Testaments say about the ordering of our loves. We are to love God and neighbor as ourselves. That trinity of relationships sums up our duties.

When a lawyer quizzed Jesus, asking him what is the greatest commandment, Jesus responded:

You shall love the Lord your God with all your heart and with all your soul and with all your mind. This is the great and first commandment. And a second is like it: You shall love your neighbor as yourself. On these two commandments depend all the Law and the Prophets. (Matt. 22:37–40)

Furthermore, the law is prefaced on God's covenantal and redemptive love: "God spoke all these words, saying, 'I am the LORD your

God, who brought you out of the land of Egypt, out of the house of slavery'" (Ex. 20:1–2).

1) "You shall have no other Gods before me" (Ex. 20:3). Israel was to worship no other gods. The inner disposition of their hearts was to be directed toward love to the one, true, eternal God. They were to acknowledge him in all they did, in their "going out and coming in," as the psalmist would express it later (Ps. 121:8). Because the foundation of the law is the one, true, and living God, the most grievous offense is treason against God. To have gods other than Yahweh is subversive idolatry.

2) "You shall not make for yourself a carved image, or any likeness of anything that is in heaven above, or that is in the earth beneath, or that is in the water under the earth. You shall not bow down to them or serve them, for I the LORD your God am a jealous God, visiting the iniquity of the fathers on the children to the third and the fourth generation of those who hate me, but showing steadfast love to thousands of those who love me and keep my commandments" (Ex. 20:4–6). As the first commandment prohibits idolatry in the broadest sense, this commandment prohibits the use of idols in worship. As the first commandment enjoins Israel to worship the true God, so this commandment enjoins them to worship him in the proper manner.

The law does not prohibit engravings, art, or imagery per se. After all, the priests' garments included images of pomegranates (Ex. 28:33–34; 39:24); the mercy seat had gold statues of cherubim (Ex. 35:18–22; 37:7); and the sanctuary was richly and vividly ornamented. The use of images was not forbidden, but worshiping those images as gods was punishable by death.

John Calvin, the Genevan Reformer, famously said, "Our minds are a perpetual factory of idols." How traitorous for us to adopt or create idols of wood, stone, or precious metals. Because of the idol worship among the nations surrounding Israel, this was a constant temptation. So much so that Moses warns them in Deuteronomy 4:15–20:

Therefore watch yourselves very carefully. Since you saw no form on the day that the LORD spoke to you at Horeb out of the midst of the fire, beware lest you act corruptly by making a carved image for yourselves, in the form of any figure, the likeness of male or female, the likeness of any animal that is on the earth, the likeness of any winged bird that flies in the air, the likeness of anything that creeps on the ground, the likeness of any fish that is in the water under the earth. And beware lest you raise your eyes to heaven, and when you see the sun and the moon and the stars, all the host of heaven, you be drawn away and bow down to them and serve them, things that the LORD your God has allotted to all the peoples under the whole heaven. But the LORD has taken you and brought you out of the iron furnace, out of Egypt, to be a people of his own inheritance, as you are this day.

God is to be loved, worshiped, and served because of his deeds and attributes, not because of his appearance. Through his attributes we see his holiness; through his deeds we see his covenant faithfulness and love. The second commandment speaks of one of those attributes as jealousy. If we worship other gods, if we serve idols, we commit spiritual adultery and provoke his jealousy. But it speaks of another of those attributes as steadfast love. Contemplating that love, Horatius Bonar wrote (in 1861) a hymn later sung at the funeral of American president Ronald Reagan:

O love of God, how strong and true!
Eternal, and yet ever new;
Uncomprehended and unbought,
Beyond all knowledge and all thought.

O love of God, how deep and great!
Far deeper than man's deepest hate;
Self-fed, self-kindled, like the light,
Changeless, eternal, infinite.

O heavenly love, how precious still,
In days of weariness and ill,

In nights of pain and helplessness,
To heal, to comfort, and to bless!

O wide embracing, wondrous love!
We read thee in the sky above,
We read thee in the earth below,
In seas that swell, and streams that flow.

We read thee best in Him who came
To bear for us the cross of shame;
Sent by the Father from on high,
Our life to live, our death to die.

We read thy power to bless and save,
E'en in the darkness of the grave;
Still more in resurrection light,
We read the fullness of thy might.

O love of God, our shield and stay
Through all the perils of our way!
Eternal love, in thee we rest
Forever safe, forever blest.

3) "You shall not take the name of the LORD your God in vain, for the LORD will not hold him guiltless who takes his name in vain" (Ex. 20:7). In this commandment God forbids profanity but not swearing, if we understand swearing to be the verbalization of our feelings of frustration or aggression. *Profanity* comes from the Latin *profanare* ("to desecrate") and *profanes* ("unholy, not consecrated"). Technically then, profanity is desecrating or using God's name in an unholy way. But the notion of taking the name of God in vain is even broader. In his remarkable devotional commentary on the Ten Commandments, Puritan theologian Thomas Watson suggests the following ways we violate this commandment:

- When we speak lightly or irreverently of God's name.
- When we profess his name but do not live consistently as his follower.

- When we use God's name flippantly in idle discourse.
- When we worship him with our lips but not with our hearts.
- When we pray to him but do not believe him.
- When we speak scornfully, jestingly, or perversely of his Word.
- When we prefix God's name to evil behavior.
- When we use our tongues to dishonor his name.
- When we make rash or unlawful vows.
- When we speak evil of God.

These are important reminders of the power of speech. No wonder the apostle James says, "If anyone thinks he is religious and does not bridle his tongue but deceives his heart, this person's religion is worthless" (James 1:26). What an extraordinarily vivid image, when one recalls that a bridle is the means of controlling a horse with its huge mass and formidable power.

4) "Remember the Sabbath day, to keep it holy. Six days you shall labor, and do all your work, but the seventh day is a Sabbath to the LORD your God. On it you shall not do any work, you, or your son, or your daughter, your male servant, or your female servant, or your livestock, or the sojourner who is within your gates. For in six days the LORD made heaven and earth, the sea, and all that is in them, and rested on the seventh day. Therefore the LORD blessed the Sabbath day and made it holy" (Ex. 20:8–11). Given its context—a largely agrarian culture—this is an extraordinarily radical commandment. We must remember that daily work, especially related to providing food and shelter, was more than a full-time job in ancient cultures. There is no evidence that most ancient people groups suffered from obesity. On the contrary, the problem was just the opposite: getting sufficient daily calories to survive. A command, therefore, to rest one day per week meant that God's people had to trust him to provide in six days what they needed for seven.

The Sabbath (*sabbat*, "to stop, cease, rest"), however, is not meant either to expose God's people to risk or to infringe on their freedom, but to liberate them from the toilsomeness of work. After all, God himself rested on the seventh day of creation. Psalm 92 is titled "A Song for the Sabbath." Pay attention to the agrarian themes in the psalm:

> It is good to give thanks to the LORD,
>   to sing praises to your name, O Most High;
> to declare your steadfast love in the morning,
>   and your faithfulness by night,
> to the music of the lute and the harp,
>   to the melody of the lyre.
> For you, O LORD, have made me glad by your work;
>   at the works of your hands I sing for joy.
>
> How great are your works, O LORD!
>   Your thoughts are very deep!
> The stupid man cannot know;
>   the fool cannot understand this:
> that though the wicked sprout like grass
>   and all evildoers flourish,
> they are doomed to destruction forever;
>   but you, O LORD, are on high forever.
> For behold, your enemies, O LORD,
>   for behold, your enemies shall perish;
>   all evildoers shall be scattered.
>
> But you have exalted my horn like that of the wild ox;
>   you have poured over me fresh oil.
> My eyes have seen the downfall of my enemies;
>   my ears have heard the doom of my evil assailants.
>
> The righteous flourish like the palm tree
>   and grow like a cedar in Lebanon.
> They are planted in the house of the LORD;
>   they flourish in the courts of our God.
> They still bear fruit in old age;
>   they are ever full of sap and green,
> to declare that the LORD is upright;
>   he is my rock, and there is no unrighteousness in him.

It is a psalm of deep delight and trust in the God who commanded the Sabbath for human flourishing. Abraham Joshua Heschel, one of the leading Jewish philosopher-theologians of the twentieth century, once said, "The Sabbath is a day for the sake of life. Man is not a beast of burden, and the Sabbath is not for the purpose of enhancing the efficiency of his work. . . . The Sabbath is not for the sake of the weekdays, the weekdays are for the sake of the Sabbath. It is not an interlude, but the climax of living."[7]

Furthermore, the Sabbath was more than a weekly observance (Exodus 20; Deuteronomy 5). In addition, every seventh year was a sabbath year (Ex. 23:10–11; Lev. 25:1–7), and every fiftieth year was a sabbath of Sabbaths, the Year of Jubilee (Lev. 25:8–12). Rest, celebration, and restoration were woven into the fabric of Israel's calendar.

THE FINAL SIX COMMANDMENTS

5) "Honor your father and your mother, that your days may be long in the land that the LORD your God is giving you" (Ex. 20:12). With this commandment there is a shift in orientation. The first four commandments had to do with Israel's relationship to God; the remaining six speak to their relationship with others. In this particular case it is the relationship between children and their parents.

Honor literally means "weighty" or "heavy." In the Old Testament the word often refers to the glory of God. It is the image C. S. Lewis used in the title of his famous sermon preached in 1942 from St. Mary's Church in Oxford, "The Weight of Glory." Children are to give due weight—value, respect, esteem—to both of their parents, father *and* mother. This was to distinguish Israel from some of the pagan nations around them. On the one hand, children were not to be allowed to become little anarchists. On the other hand, stern patriarchy that treated wives more like children than like equals was also prohibited. We see this again in Proverbs 1:8–9: "Hear, my son, your father's instruction, and forsake not

---

[7] Abraham Joshua Heschel, *The Sabbath* (New York: Farrar Straus Giroux, 2005), 2.

your mother's teaching, for they are a graceful garland for your head and pendants for your neck."

The Bible teaches that under God, lines of authority begin in the family. That is why there are such severe penalties associated with incorrigible disobedience:

> Anyone who curses his father or his mother shall surely be put to death; he has cursed his father or his mother; his blood is upon him. (Lev. 20:9)

> If a man has a stubborn and rebellious son who will not obey the voice of his father or the voice of his mother, and, though they discipline him, will not listen to them, then his father and his mother shall take hold of him and bring him out to the elders of his city at the gate of the place where he lives, and they shall say to the elders of his city, "This our son is stubborn and rebellious; he will not obey our voice; he is a glutton and a drunkard." Then all the men of the city shall stone him to death with stones. So you shall purge the evil from your midst, and all Israel shall hear, and fear. (Deut. 21:18–21)

It is also true that great blessing belongs to those who honor their parents: "Your days may be long in the land that the LORD your God is giving you." Again, Proverbs echoes this commandment and the results of obedience: "My son, do not forget my teaching, but let your heart keep my commandments, for length of days and years of life and peace they will add to you" (Prov. 3:1–2).

6) "You shall not murder" (Ex. 20:13). In the Hebrew this commandment comes in the form of the terse expression "never murder." To understand it as the King James Version puts it, "Do not kill," is not only to make it too expansive but to make the Bible self-contradictory. There are circumstances in which killing might be just and defensible, but murder has no defense. No Israelite acting privately had the right to take another human life. Only proper authorities had that right.

The people of God are not to be a brutal people. Unlike the peoples around her, Israel was a lawful nation. Moreover, she was a people meant to live under the principle of proportional justice. Many critics of the Bible suggest that its "eye-for-an-eye" form of justice was an expression of primitive harshness. In fact, the principle was exceedingly civilizing when set against other ancient forms of justice where revenge, feuds, and retaliation were the norm. Israel's system of justice was the origin of the West's notion that the punishment is to fit the crime. Rather than authorizing brutality, it prevents disproportionality. In some cultures, stealing could mean the death penalty. But in Israel, no *more* than an eye for an eye was permissible. And even then, only the proper authorities had the power to punish evildoers. Justice was neither arbitrary nor vicious.

Positively, the commandment never to murder protected the sanctity of every human life. Israel was fully aware of the fact that, following the great flood, God reestablished his covenant with Noah, his family, and with all subsequent humanity:

> God blessed Noah and his sons and said to them, "Be fruitful and multiply and fill the earth. The fear of you and the dread of you shall be upon every beast of the earth and upon every bird of the heavens, upon everything that creeps on the ground and all the fish of the sea. Into your hand they are delivered. Every moving thing that lives shall be food for you. And as I gave you the green plants, I give you everything. But you shall not eat flesh with its life, that is, its blood. And for your lifeblood I will require a reckoning: from every beast I will require it and from man. From his fellow man I will require a reckoning for the life of man. Whoever sheds the blood of man, by man shall his blood be shed, for God made man in his own image" (Gen. 9:1–6).

Just as with the original covenant God had made, here again his human creations are to be fruitful and multiply and to exercise dominion-stewardship. Here, clear permission is given to kill animals for food, but because man is made in God's image, unjustly killing another human being is explicitly prohibited. As John Calvin wrote, "Our neighbor bears the image of God: to use him, abuse him, or misuse him is to do violence to the person of God who images himself in every human soul, the Fall notwithstanding. . . . Not only do I despise my flesh when I wish to oppress someone, but I violate the image of God which is in me."

7) "You shall not commit adultery" (Ex. 20:14). Because sex is a wonderful gift of God meant to be expressed within the context of the one-flesh union of marriage, promiscuity is an especially egregious offense. Marital fidelity is to mark God's people. A rightly ordered society depended on stable heterosexual marriages, and still does.

Even though polygamy was tolerated during some periods of Israel's history, monogamy was always considered the ideal. The creation mandate was "a man" and "his wife" (Gen. 2:24). Cohabitation, incest, bestiality, and other violations of that ideal were explicitly banned.

Both Jesus and Paul reaffirmed and reinforced the marriage covenant. Before repudiating divorce except for sexual promiscuity, Jesus said, "Have you not read that he who created them from the beginning made them male and female, and said, 'Therefore a man shall leave his father and his mother and hold fast to his wife, and the two shall become one flesh'? So they are no longer two but one flesh. What therefore God has joined together, let not man separate" (Matt. 19:4–6). Likewise, the apostle Paul said that the marital union—in which "a man shall leave his father and mother and hold fast to his wife, and the two shall become one flesh" (Eph. 5:31)—described analogously the union of Christ with his church.

In his great apologetic for the faith, *Mere Christianity*, C. S. Lewis, who married later in life, famously wrote:

> The Christian idea of marriage is based on Christ's words that a man and wife are to be regarded as a single organism—for

that is what the words "one flesh" would be in modern English. And the Christians believe that when He said this He was not expressing a sentiment but stating a fact—just as one is stating a fact when one says that a lock and its key are one mechanism, or that a violin and a bow are one musical instrument. The inventor of the human machine was telling us that its two halves, the male and the female, were made to be combined together in pairs, not simply on the sexual level, but totally combined. The monstrosity of sexual intercourse outside marriage is that those who indulge in it are trying to isolate one kind of union (the sexual) from all the other kinds of union which were intended to go along with it and make up the total union. The Christian attitude does not mean that there is anything wrong about sexual pleasure, any more than about the pleasure of eating. It means that you must not isolate that pleasure and try to get it by itself, any more than you ought to try to get the pleasures of taste without swallowing and digesting, by chewing things and spitting them out again.[8]

8) "You shall not steal" (Ex. 20:15). To steal is to take that which belongs to another. By implication, this commandment affirms that ownership of personal property is permissible, since one cannot take what does not already belong to someone else. To be sure, contemporary concepts of property differ in some ways from those of ancient Judaism and Christianity, but the idea that one could justly own property derives from Judeo-Christian principles. The eighth commandment would be meaningless without the notion of private property. And what one may own, one may sell, trade, or give away. The general rule is applied throughout the Torah to specific cases, from stealing oxen to money to security deposits to slaves (Ex. 22:1–16; Lev. 6:2–5; 19:11–13; Deut. 24:7).

Furthermore, Scripture teaches that the antidote to stealing is not merely not stealing but working for the purposes of sharing. Paul writes to the Ephesian church, "Let the thief no longer steal,

---

[8] C. S. Lewis, *Mere Christianity* (New York: Macmillan, 1952), 95–96.

but rather let him labor, doing honest work with his own hands, so that he may have something to share with anyone in need" (Eph. 4:28). Generosity is to replace pilfering.

9) "You shall not bear false witness against your neighbor" (Ex. 20:16). This is the first of the commandments to explicitly invoke responsibilities to one's neighbor. Commentators point out that the word *neighbor* in this case is a legal term. Its use implies that courts are legitimate places to adjudicate disputes and that giving false testimony is morally blameworthy. Leviticus 5:1 makes clear that failure to divulge what one knows in a court of law is also a violation of the commandment. Sins of omission may be as grievous as sins of commission.

What is true in a legal sense here is also true in a more general sense. The law says, "You shall not steal; you shall not deal falsely; you shall not lie to one another" (Lev. 19:11). And Jesus taught that everyone is our neighbor. The foundations of business require basic trust among members of society. Social stability depends on obedience to these commandments.

10) "You shall not covet your neighbor's house; you shall not covet your neighbor's wife, or his male servant, or his female servant, or his ox, or his donkey, or anything that is your neighbor's" (Ex. 20:17). The commandments are not only aimed at behavior but are also meant to regulate desires. Not only is stealing wrong, but *wanting* someone else's property is wrong. A good society is not only one in which people obey the law but one in which people want to obey it. After all, people may indeed follow the law under tyrannical rulers, but their obedience is a consequence of fear, not love for neighbor.

The apostle Paul understood the intent of the law when he said, "For the commandments, 'You shall not commit adultery, You shall not murder, You shall not steal, You shall not covet,' and any other commandment, are summed up in this word: 'You shall love your neighbor as yourself.' Love does no wrong to a neighbor;

therefore love is the fulfilling of the law" (Rom. 13:9–10). Neighbor love delights when others flourish.

Against the backdrop of contemporary multiculturalism, it is easy to underestimate the role the Ten Commandments have played in the development of Western ethics, law, policy, and culture. The Ten Commandments are a cornerstone in that tradition. United States president Harry Truman put it this way:

> The fundamental basis of this nation's laws was given to Moses on the Mount. The fundamental basis of our Bill of Rights comes from the teachings we get from Exodus and St. Matthew, from Isaiah and St. Paul. I don't think we emphasize that enough these days. If we don't have a proper fundamental moral background, we will finally end up with a totalitarian government which does not believe in rights for anybody except the State![9]

The source of the law in any culture is the deity of that culture. In Israel it was clear that the source was the one true and living God. The Ten Commandments reflect the nature of God as holy, loving, truth-loving, honest, and pure. Those are the attributes of any decent society. To the degree that a society repudiates or neglects those ideals, to that degree the society erodes to chaos. As celebrated British historian Arnold J. Toynbee put it, "Civilisations die from suicide, not murder."[10]

---

[9] Harry S. Truman, February 15, 1950, at 10:05 a.m., in an address given to the Attorney General's Conference on Law Enforcement Problems in the Department of Justice Auditorium, Washington, DC; organizations present included the Department of Justice, the National Association of Attorneys, the United States Conference of Lawyers, and the National Institute of Municipal Law Officers. Public Papers of the Presidents: Harry S. Truman, 1950, Containing Public Messages, Speeches, and Statements of the President, January 1 to December 31, 1950 (Washington, DC: United States Government Printing Office, 1965), Item 37, p. 157. http://trumanlibrary.org/public papers/viewpapers.php?pid=657.
[10] Arnold J. Toynbee, *A Study of History: Abridgement of Volumes I to VI* (Oxford: Oxford University Press, 1947), 273.

✙ 3

THE HISTORY OF MORAL REASONING, PART 2

Princeton anthropology professor Clifford Geertz once defined *culture* as "simply the ensemble of stories we tell ourselves about ourselves."[1] If that is even half true, then Western culture has been shaped significantly by the story of Hebrew religion, from the creation account to the Ten Commandments, and from the historical covenants to the fiery pronouncements of the prophets. But Western culture, including Western morality, has been most profoundly influenced by Jesus of Nazareth and New Testament Christianity. Today, however, as my colleague and New Testament scholar George Guthrie warns, "The Bible is in a slow fade from our collective conversation, not only in the realm of spiritual and church life but also in the realms of politics, social institutions, literature, and the arts."[2] We should ask ourselves, especially in a relativist culture, what are the costs of our historical amnesia?

Who is Jesus?

Why do Christians look to Jesus of Nazareth for moral instruction instead of the Buddha, Confucius, or Hallmark cards? There are many great men of the past. What makes Jesus's teaching authoritative? The answer to that question has to be: "On account of who he is." Who is Jesus? That is an ancient question with ur-

---

[1] Clifford Geertz, *The Interpretation of Cultures* (New York: Basic, 1973), 448.
[2] George Guthrie, *Read the Bible for Life* (Nashville: Broadman, 2011), 8.

gent contemporary relevance. As a matter of fact, Jesus himself was curious about who people thought he was:

> When Jesus came into the district of Caesarea Philippi, he asked his disciples, "Who do people say that the Son of Man is?" And they said, "Some say John the Baptist, others say Elijah, and others Jeremiah or one of the prophets." He said to them, "But who do you say that I am?" Simon Peter replied, "You are the Christ, the Son of the living God." And Jesus answered him, "Blessed are you, Simon Bar-Jonah! For flesh and blood has not revealed this to you, but my Father who is in heaven." (Matt. 16:13–17)

The Christ, the anointed one, the promised Messiah—that's how Peter answered that question. And who is Messiah? The Son of God, God in human flesh. It is because of who he is that Jesus and his teaching come with such authoritative force. "We have to do with God himself as we have to do with this man. God himself speaks when this man speaks in human speech," said theologian Karl Barth.[3] Since Christ is God, his followers must attend to what he said about the true, the good, and the beautiful.

THE SERMON ON THE MOUNT

Probably no New Testament ethical passage has received as much attention as the Sermon on the Mount, most likely because no section of the Bible concentrates as much of the moral teaching of Jesus. The sermon has even worked its way into pop culture. "Blessed are the peacemakers," "salt of the earth," "no one can serve two masters," and "do unto others," are expressions frequently heard in everyday conversation.

In addition to its rich ethical content, the Sermon on the Mount reveals the transition from the old covenant to the new covenant. Because of its importance, the sermon appears more frequently than any other three chapters of the Bible in the writings of the

---

[3] Karl Barth, *The Doctrine of Reconciliation*, trans. G. W. Bromiley, vol. 4, part 2, *Church Dogmatics*, ed. Geoffrey W. Bromiley and Thomas E. Torrance (Edinburgh: T. & T. Clark, 1960), 51.

early church. As Robert Guelich puts it in his helpful commentary on the Sermon on the Mount,

> From the Didache to Chrysostom, the Sermon offered, on the one hand, a classical expression of Christian ethics, the guide for Christian conduct, with little or no question about how such "impossible" demands could be carried out in an immoral world. On the other hand, the Sermon material, especially 5:17–48, became a major apologetic basis for countering the theological heresy from Marcion to the Manichaeans that interpreted Jesus and the New Testament against a radical break with Judaism and the Old Testament.[4]

THE BEATITUDES: TRUE HAPPINESS

As we shall continue to see throughout this book, one of the burdens of an ethical theory is to define what happiness is. This is because everyone is agreed that happiness has an important connection to our moral lives. Some say it is pleasure, others say it is duty, and still others claim it is completing one's projects. Each theorist has a slightly different description of human happiness.

Beatitude comes from the family of words that is translated as "blessed," sometimes as "happy" (TEV) or "how happy" (PHILLIPS). Indeed, the word carries a congratulatory character and should be taken as "fortunate," "to be congratulated," or "supremely happy." In the Beatitudes Jesus describes the life of happiness:

> And he opened his mouth and taught them, saying:
> "Blessed are the poor in spirit, for theirs is the kingdom of heaven.
> "Blessed are those who mourn, for they shall be comforted.
> "Blessed are the meek, for they shall inherit the earth.
> "Blessed are those who hunger and thirst for righteousness, for they shall be satisfied.

---

[4] Robert Guelich, *The Sermon on the Mount: A Foundation for Understanding* (Dallas: Word, 1982), 14.

"Blessed are the merciful, for they shall receive mercy.

"Blessed are the pure in heart, for they shall see God.

"Blessed are the peacemakers, for they shall be called sons of God.

"Blessed are those who are persecuted for righteousness' sake, for theirs is the kingdom of heaven.

"Blessed are you when others revile you and persecute you and utter all kinds of evil against you falsely on my account. Rejoice and be glad, for your reward is great in heaven, for so they persecuted the prophets who were before you." (Matt. 5:2–12)

Those who heard Jesus would have known that he did not invent these Beatitudes. They would doubtless have heard the echo from one of the best known Messianic texts of the Old Testament, Isaiah 61:1–3:

> The Spirit of the Lord GOD is upon me,
>   because the LORD has anointed me
> to bring good news to the poor;
>   he has sent me to bind up the brokenhearted,
> to proclaim liberty to the captives,
>   and the opening of the prison to those who are bound;
> to proclaim the year of the LORD's favor,
>   and the day of vengeance of our God;
>   to comfort all who mourn;
> to grant to those who mourn in Zion—
>   to give them a beautiful headdress instead of ashes,
> the oil of gladness instead of mourning,
>   the garment of praise instead of a faint spirit;
> that they may be called oaks of righteousness,
>   the planting of the LORD, that he may be glorified.

The Beatitudes, therefore, describe the virtues and character of those for whom the long-awaited Messiah has come. They are poor in spirit and dependent on God, not on themselves or others. They are mourners for whom Jesus is their consolation. They are meek, marked by humility, gentleness, and nonaggression. They are hungry and thirsty for righteousness, desperately seeking to live in a right relationship with God. They are merciful, because they have been recipients of God's mercy. They are pure in heart, a people whose singleness of devotion shapes their behavior in every way. Much more than being nonaggressive, they are peacemakers who work for *shalom* ("holistic peace," "completeness"). Finally, they suffer insults humbly and patiently.

New Testament scholar Craig Blomberg concludes:

> The upshot of the Beatitudes is a complete inversion of the attitude popularly known in our culture as "machismo." In fact, this attitude is not limited to a particular culture but characterizes humanity's self-centered, self-arrogating pride which invariably seeks personal security and survival above the good of others. We are enabled to invert natural, worldly values only when we recognize that God will in turn invert our marginalized status and grant eternal compensation. This is not to promote works-righteousness; Jesus is addressing those already professing discipleship (5:1). But, like James among the Epistles, Matthew is the one Gospel to emphasize most the changed life that must flow from commitment to Christ.[5]

The Sermon on the Mount is, therefore, a potent remedy for what we might call "Christian legalism." Disciples are marked by virtuous living, not by rigid rule following, thinking they can somehow please God through their performance. Jesus came to transform the character of his followers, not to make them better Pharisees. Their form of life makes a decided difference in the culture—they are like salt, an antiseptic and preservative, and like light, to illuminate the darkness. Note that Jesus uses moral language when he speaks of their "good works." He tells his disciples that all of this is to be true of them so that others may see their good works and give glory to their Father who is in heaven (Matt. 5:16).

The remainder of the sermon is meant to affirm and deepen

---

[5] Craig Blomberg, *Matthew*, New American Commentary (Nashville: Broadman, 1992), 102.

Jesus's followers' understanding of the moral law, since Jesus came to fulfill it, not abolish it. Says Blomberg, "All of the Old Testament remains normative and relevant for Jesus's followers (2 Tim. 3:16), but none of it can be rightly interpreted until one understands how it has been fulfilled in Christ. Every Old Testament text must be viewed in light of Jesus's person and ministry and the changes introduced by the covenant he inaugurated."[6]

Jesus teaches them what new-covenant life is like. He gives instructions about ethical issues including anger (Matt. 5:21–26), sexual desire (vv. 27–30), oath taking (v. 33), retaliation (vv. 38–42), and loving one's enemies (vv. 43–48). In Matthew 6 Jesus addresses true versus hypocritical piety (v. 1), almsgiving (vv. 2–4), prayer (vv. 5–15), fasting (vv. 16–18), money (vv. 19–24), and anxiety (vv. 25–34). In the final section of the sermon, Matthew 7, he calls them to charitable assessment of others (vv. 1–6), persistence in prayer (vv. 7–11), obedience to the Golden Rule (vv. 12–14), watchfulness (vv. 15–20), and avoiding presumption (vv. 21–23).

In his concluding remarks (7:24–27) Jesus describes the wise person as someone who hears and obeys what he says. Since he is God, a form of divine-command ethic seems to be implied.

THE VIRTUES AND NATURAL LAW

At least since the mid-300s BC, Greek philosophy under the influence of Aristotle taught a virtue theory of ethics. Aristotle wanted to understand the aim of human life. Why are we here? What is our purpose? He explored a number of alternatives. Perhaps the end, or what he called the *telos*, of human life was pleasure. People seem to be highly motivated to avoid pain and achieve pleasure. But, no, thought Aristotle, people do indeed seek pleasure, but they do so because they think it leads to something else. Might that goal be wealth? Again, most people seem to enjoy possessions—houses, money, land, etc. But even when they acquire them, they still lack

---

[6] Ibid., 104.

something. The acquisition of "stuff" does not seem to satisfy for very long. Finally, he suggests that perhaps people find their purpose in fame and honor. Many people are self-seeking, to be sure. They enjoy fame for a season, but it does not seem to be an *ultimate* purpose or goal. People want fame because they believe it leads to something else. What is that for which pleasure, wealth, and fame are sought?

After a great deal of searching, Aristotle arrived at an answer: the *telos* of human life is happiness. Not a giddy, flippant, hilarious kind of happiness but a deeply satisfying, holistic happiness. The end for humans is what Aristotle called *eudaimonia. Eudaimonia* is sometimes translated "human flourishing." Happiness for Aristotle was a sense of well-being and completeness, perhaps something like what the Hebrew Scriptures meant by *shalom.* How could individuals achieve this happiness? It is achieved by living deeply human lives; for human beings, unlike the other animals, have a rational soul or rational aspect to their natures. When humans follow their *telos*, they come closer to *eudaimonia* by cultivating the virtues or excellences of the soul.

A virtue is a human potential that becomes part of who a human being is by exercise, just as an athlete trains so she can run or swim consistently with her nature as a runner or swimmer. We become virtuous, said Aristotle, through practices that develop in us the character or habit of doing the good. The best way to understand the virtues, according to Aristotle, is to see them in the lived experience of virtuous people, those who have developed virtuous habits.

Interestingly, Aristotle's discussion of the virtues began with courage, the Golden Mean between soldierly cowardice and recklessness. Thus, we learn about courage in the stories of how Diomedes and Hektor exemplified the virtue of courage. In the Aristotelian tradition the cardinal virtues were courage, justice, temperance, and wisdom. In contrast, in the Christian tradition the cardinal virtues are faith, hope, and love.

The "angelic doctor," Thomas Aquinas (1225–1274), is probably best known for bringing those of the Aristotelian tradition and those of the Christian tradition into conversation with one another. His massive *Summa Theologiae* is, in some ways, Aquinas's attempt to answer Tertullian's famous question, "What has Athens to do with Jerusalem?" At question 69, on the Beatitudes, Aquinas asks whether the beatitudes differ from the virtues. After considering several objections, Thomas concludes:

> *I answer that*, As we have stated above, happiness is the last end of human life. Now one is said to possess the end already when one hopes to possess it; and therefore the Philosopher [Aristotle] says that children are said to be happy because they are full of hope; and the Apostle says (Rom. Viii. 24): We are saved by hope. Again, we hope to obtain an end because we are suitably moved towards that end and approach thereto; and this takes place through some action. Now a man is moved towards the end which is happiness, and approaches to it by works of virtue, and above all by the works of the gifts, if we speak of eternal happiness, for which our reason is not sufficient, since we need to be moved by the Holy Ghost, and to be perfected with His gifts that we may obey and follow him. Consequently, the beatitudes differ from the virtues and gifts, not as habit from habit, but as an act from a habit.

From the time of Plato, Aristotle, and the Stoics, natural-law ethics has flourished among Christians and some non-Christians. In his *Summa Theologiae*, Thomas Aquinas defended what he believed to be a distinctly Christian expression of the natural law. Although God's revelation, both in his Son and in the Bible, are ultimate and necessary sources of moral authority, according to Aquinas, the principles of practical reason are "known through themselves to all."[7] That is, the principles of practical reason are available and self-evident to everyone.

---

[7] Thomas Aquinas, *Summa Theologiae*, 1-1, q. 94, a. 2.

For instance, in some US states motorcyclists must wear helmets when riding their bikes. Not all states have chosen the same requirement. But this is merely a matter of law, of legal convention. However, the notion that life is a basic good does not depend on a convention, nor is it only true in some states. We all know the truth of the matter through practical reason, which all of us share. Human life is a basic good, not least because without life existence is impossible. Thus, life is a "natural" good.

To claim that there is a "natural law" is to claim that there is a normative moral order governed by that law, not by mere convention or mutual agreement. Furthermore, the claim entails that normative morality is discovered, not constructed. This is seen most clearly perhaps in the first principle of practical reason, namely, "what is good ought to be pursued, what is bad avoided." If one knows what the words *good* and *bad* mean in ordinary language, then anyone can know the principle to be true.

It is worth pointing out that in his masterful manifesto for civil rights, *Letter from a Birmingham Jail*, Martin Luther King Jr. explicitly invoked the natural-law tradition:

> How does one determine whether a law is just or unjust? A just law is a man-made code that squares with the moral law or the law of God. An unjust law is a code that is out of harmony with the moral law. To put it in the terms of St. Thomas Aquinas: An unjust law is a human law that is not rooted in eternal law and natural law. Any law that uplifts human personality is just. Any law that degrades human personality is unjust.

In his 1993 encyclical (a circular letter) *Veritatis Splendor*, Pope John Paul II expressed natural-law ethics in a rich and enduring way. Despite human depravity and sinfulness,

> no darkness of error or of sin can totally take away from man the light of God the Creator. In the depths of his heart there always remains a yearning for absolute truth and a thirst to at-

tain full knowledge of it. This is eloquently proved by man's tireless search for knowledge in all fields. It is proved even more by his search for the meaning of life. The development of science and technology, this splendid testimony of the human capacity for understanding and for perseverance, does not free humanity from the obligation to ask the ultimate religious questions. Rather, it spurs us on to face the most painful and decisive of struggles, those of the heart and of the moral conscience.

. . . No one can escape from the fundamental questions: What must I do? How do I distinguish good from evil? The answer is only possible thanks to the splendour of the truth which shines forth deep within the human spirit, as the Psalmist bears witness: "There are many who say: 'O that we might see some good! Let the light of your face shine on us, O Lord'" (Ps 4:6).[8]

Because of his confidence in God's deposit of truth in the world and the human capacity to perceive that truth, John Paul called on his readers to reject relativism and embrace the Catholic Church's moral teaching. Rooted in human nature and shared by all humankind, the natural law is accessible to both Christian and non-Christian. "Inasmuch as the natural law expresses the dignity of the human person and lays the foundation for his fundamental right and duties, it is universal in its precepts and its authority extends to all mankind."[9]

There are many things to commend in *Veritatis Splendor* and the natural-law tradition. Historically, the natural-law tradition has been thought of as representative of Catholic moral theology. Today the natural-law tradition is alive and well among Protestant evangelicals as well. Penned before he converted to Catholicism, J. Budziszewski's *Written on the Heart: The Case for Natural Law* is a very helpful introduction to natural-law thought.[10] J. Daryl

---

[8] John Paul II, *Veritatis Splendor*, Encyclical Regarding Certain Fundamental Questions of the Church's Moral Teaching, August 6, 1993, para. 1–2. http://www.vatican.va/holy_father/john_paul_ii/encyclicals/documents/hf_jp-ii_enc_06081993_veritatis-splendor_en.html.

[9] Ibid., section 51.

[10] J. Budziszewski, *Written on the Heart: The Case for Natural Law* (Downers Grove, IL: IVP Academic, 1997).

Charles's, *Retrieving Natural Law: A Return to Moral First Things*;[11] David Van Drunen's, *Natural Law and the Two Kingdoms: A Study in the Development of Reformed Social Thought*;[12] and *Natural Law and Evangelical Political Thought*, edited by Jesse Covington, Bryan McGraw, and Micah Watson, are also helpful evangelical treatments of the topic.[13]

Some Protestants, while appreciative of the contribution of natural-law thinking, worry that the natural-law approach does not take seriously enough the effects of human sinfulness on human perception and the moral blindness that results from sin. They believe that through common grace and general revelation, God has indeed made some things known to us. But even those truths revealed through common grace are rejected by sinful individuals. So Paul says,

> The wrath of God is revealed from heaven against all ungodliness and unrighteousness of men, who by their unrighteousness suppress the truth. For what can be known about God is plain to them, because God has shown it to them. For his invisible attributes, namely, his eternal power and divine nature, have been clearly perceived, ever since the creation of the world, in the things that have been made. So they are without excuse. For although they knew God, they did not honor him as God or give thanks to him, but they became futile in their thinking, and their foolish hearts were darkened. Claiming to be wise, they became fools, and exchanged the glory of the immortal God for images resembling mortal man and birds and animals and creeping things. (Rom. 1:18–23)

In light of what Paul says, many Protestants, especially from Reformed and Baptistic traditions, place less confidence in the

---

[11] J. Daryl Charles, *Retrieving Natural Law: A Return to Moral First Things* (Grand Rapids, MI: Eerdmans, 2008).

[12] David Van Drunen, *Natural Law and the Two Kingdoms: A Study in the Development of Reformed Social Thought* (Grand Rapids, MI: Eerdmans, 2010).

[13] Jesse Covington, Bryan McGraw, Micah Watson, eds., *Natural Law and Evangelical Political Thought* (New York: Lexington, 2012).

power of human reason for moral knowledge and more confidence in scriptural revelation. These Protestant thinkers believe human reason is an important means for discerning truth but are less optimistic about its results because of the noetic effects of the fall. Examples of more biblically grounded ethics include John Jefferson Davis, *Evangelical Ethics: Issues Facing the Church Today*;[14] Scott Rae, *Moral Choices: An Introduction to Ethics*;[15] Kyle Fedler, *Exploring Christian Ethics: Biblical Foundations for Morality*;[16] and John Feinberg and Paul Feinberg, *Ethics for a Brave New World*.[17]

---

[14] John Jefferson Davis, *Evangelical Ethics: Issues Facing the Church Today*, 3rd ed. (Phillipsburg, NJ: P&R, 2004).
[15] Scott Rae, *Moral Choices: An Introduction to Ethics*, 3rd ed. (Grand Rapids, MI: Zondervan, 2009).
[16] Kyle D. Fedler, *Exploring Christian Ethics: Biblical Foundations for Morality* (Louisville, KY: Westminster, 2006).
[17] John S. Feinberg and Paul D. Feinberg, *Ethics for a Brave New World*, 2nd ed. (Wheaton, IL: Crossway, 2010).

4

ENLIGHTENMENT ETHICS

Can we be good without God and his revelation? Many thinkers of the Enlightenment thought so. The religious wars in Europe from the sixteenth to eighteenth centuries did not leave people flush with confidence that agreement on faith, ethics, and politics was possible. The Enlightenment or age of reason was in many ways a response to this dilemma. The period of history we call "the Enlightenment" was marked by dependence on human reason rather than on divine revelation as the foundation for morality.

KANT AND PRINCIPLISM

One of the architects of the Enlightenment was Immanuel Kant (1724–1804), who was born and lived his entire life in Koenigsberg, Prussia (present-day Germany). After working as a private tutor, he returned to complete his university education at thirty-one years of age and became a professor at forty-six. He was a very regimented individual. It was said that the shopkeepers set their watches by the time each day that Professor Kant strolled by. A busy professor, some weeks he gave as many as twenty-six lectures.

Later in his career he formulated his "critical philosophy" in three formidable volumes: *The Critique of Pure Reason* (1781), *The Critique of Practical Reason* (1788), and the *Critique of Judgment* (1790). He considered his own work in philosophy to be equivalent to the Copernican revolution in cosmology.

Kant published his *Groundwork of the Metaphysic of Morals* in 1785 as an attempt "to seek out and establish the supreme principle of morality" on the basis of pure reason alone.[1] Kant defines his notion of the good in his very first sentence: "It is impossible to conceive anything at all in the world, or even out of it, which can be taken as good without qualification, except a good will."[2] Not fame, wealth, honor, health, or even happiness count as good without qualification, since each is sought for the benefits it brings. Only the will to do the good is good for its own sake.

Happiness is not unimportant. It is even desirable, according to Kant. So happiness has some utility, but it is not the purpose of reason to make us happy. The purpose of reason, argued Kant, is to produce a good will. What is a good will? It is one that acts for the sake of duty. When a cashier gives a customer correct change, she is acting in accordance with duty, for it is her duty to do so.

Duty is, therefore, acting in such a way that everyone can follow the same law and do their duty. In order to test our duties to see if they are in fact obligatory, Kant said we should follow what he called the "Categorical Imperative." This imperative has several different formulations in *The Groundwork*, the first of which is, "Act only on that maxim through which you can at the same time will that it should become a universal law."[3] In other words, if it is *my* duty to do this or that, it must also be *someone else's* duty to do the same. The principle should be universalize-able; that is, it should apply to everyone.

Kant enumerated several duties as examples. Suicide, telling false promises, not using one's talents, and not sharing with those in hardship were examined to see if they could count as duties. To illustrate how the Categorical Imperative works as a test for one's duty, here is what Kant said about lying:

---

[1] Immanuel Kant, *Groundwork of the Metaphysic of Morals*, trans. H. J. Paton (New York: Harper Torchbooks, 1964), 60.
[2] Ibid., 61.
[3] Ibid., 70.

Another finds himself driven to borrowing money because of need. He well knows that he will not be able to pay it back; but he sees too that he will get no loan unless he gives a firm promise to pay it back within a fixed time. He is inclined to make such a promise; but he has still enough conscience to ask "Is it not unlawful and contrary to duty to get out of difficulties in this way?" Supposing, however, he did resolve to do so, the maxim of his action would run thus: "Whenever I believe myself short of money, I will borrow money and promise to pay it back, though I know that this will never be done." Now this principle of self-love or personal advantage is perhaps quite compatible with my own entire future welfare; only there remains the question "Is it right?" I therefore transform the demand of self-love into a universal law and frame my question thus: "How would things stand if my maxim became a universal law?" I then see straight away that this maxim can never rank as a universal law of nature and be self-consistent, but must necessarily contradict itself. For the universality of a law that every one believing himself to be in need can make any promise he pleases with the intention not to keep it would make promising, and the very purpose of promising, itself impossible, since no one would believe he was being promised anything, but would laugh at utterances of this kind as empty shams.[4]

According to Kant, then, it is never morally permissible to tell a lie. On the surface this may seem reasonable and straightforward. Upon reflection, Kant's view raises significant concerns. For instance, were those righteous Gentile Christians in Hitler's Germany wrong when they lied about hiding Jews to protect them? When a patient asks her doctor plaintively, "Do I have, um, cancer?" must the doctor always and immediately respond yes, whether or not he senses the woman is prepared for the news? What about espionage to protect innocent people from tyrannical leaders or to spy on drug cartels? In other words, might there be some conditions, however rare, under which it is one's duty to tell a lie? If just one exception is possible, Kant's entire system is at risk.

---

[4] Ibid., 89–90.

Furthermore, following the critique of the late Oxford moral philosopher Philippa Foot, at best Kant's method generates rules of etiquette but not moral duties. Can we make it a universal law that people tie their left shoe before they tie their right one? Of course. Few, if any, individuals would want to grant, however, that the order in which one ties one's shoes is either right or wrong. It's simply not a moral issue. So perhaps Kant's theory does not do the work he wanted it to do, argued Foot.

Another important Kantian corollary came in the form of the practical imperative Kant stated this way: "Act in such a way that you always treat humanity, whether in your own person or in the person of any other, never simply as a means, but always at the same time as an end."[5] In other words, human beings are ends in themselves and may never be used to attain someone else's purposes. Historically, this may be Kant's most famous axiom, finding its way into discussions about human dignity, personal autonomy, and informed consent. Even this imperative is not without its problems, however. Because Kant valued reason so much, he granted that only a "rational being" is an end in himself or herself. What about unborn human beings whose rational capacity is not yet functional? What about someone who has lost her rational capacity through a brain injury or Alzheimer's? Do we have no duties to them? It appears that Kant's theory would say we do not. We have only a duty not to harm them because of their symbolic status. That is, we should not harm animals or nonrational humans because it would make us callous to our duties to rational humans.

Much of what we consider morally praiseworthy conduct is either ruled out as morally worthless or merely unimportant for Kant. For instance, compassion, love, sympathy, and other virtues seem to be entirely missing in his account. His theory is about duty, duty, and more duty! Finally, Kant believed that even God must conform to the requirements of reason. God is not, therefore,

---

[5] Ibid., 96.

the giver of the moral law. There is no more goodness in doing what God commands than there is goodness for doing something to avoid pain and enjoy pleasure. The good is found solely in doing what reason demands.

BENTHAM, MILL, AND UTILITARIANISM

Another Enlightenment approach to ethics, utilitarianism, was inspired by Jeremy Bentham (1768–1832) and the son of one of his collaborators, John Stuart Mill (1806–1873). Bentham was what philosophers call a psychological hedonist. That is, he believed that human beings are ruled by the principles of pleasure and pain. Pleasure is good; pain is bad. Moreover, people are naturally selfish since they seek their own pleasure over that of others. Thus, the greatest good is to maximize pleasure and minimize pain for the greatest number of persons. Since pleasure and pain were said to have "utility" in making moral decisions, Bentham and Mill are known as utilitarians. According to Bentham, pleasures and pains differ only in seven ways:

- Intensity
- Duration
- Certainty
- Propinquity (nearness or farness in time)
- Fecundity
- Purity
- Extent

Bentham also thought that one could measure these criteria in strictly quantitative ways, assigning numerical values to each criterion. He is known, therefore, as a "quantitative hedonist." Pleasurable experiences could be ranked on a scale of how much pleasure they gave (intensity), for how long (duration), and whether the experience of pleasure was closer or farther in time (propinquity), etc.

Bentham's famous axiom, "pushpin is as poetry," suggests that one kind of pleasure is the same as another kind of pleasure. Push-pin, a child's game, resulted in pleasure, and poetry gave pleasure. Pleasure is pleasure; pain is pain. And one person's pleasures and pains are the same as another person's pleasures and pains. They differ only in quantity along the lines described above. Because Bentham thought this was the case, he believed we could assign numerical values to pleasures and pains and create a "hedonic calculus" for determining whether a decision resulted in greater pleasure or greater pain. The consequences of a good act should produce less pain and more pleasure.

Should you tell a lie in a given situation? Run the numbers. On a scale of 1 to 10, where 1 is great pain and 10 is great pleasure, will the falsehood result in greater pleasure? If so, not only are you permitted to lie, but also you are morally *obligated* to tell the lie. If the lie causes more pain than pleasure, you are obligated not to tell the lie.

Interestingly, because Bentham thought that the good was defined by pleasures and pains and nothing else, he had no place for natural rights. Thus, he favored the French Revolution but was against the reasons given for it, namely, that by virtue of his or her humanity every person has a right to life, liberty, and the pursuit of happiness. The idea of natural rights was nonsense to Bentham. Life, liberty, property, security, and other basic human rights were not grounded in nature or nature's God but purely in whether they resulted in the greatest happiness for the greatest number where happiness is defined as pleasure. This exposed utilitarianism to a critique that we will explore next with respect to John Stuart Mill.

Though Mill agreed with Bentham that good and bad should be defined in terms of pleasure and pain, he differed with his merely quantitative approach. Mill maintained that pleasures and pains could also be measured qualitatively. "There are many qualities of agreeable feeling we call pleasure, not just one," said Mill in *Utilitarianism* (1863), his classic on the subject. Because of their higher faculties, human beings are more sensitive to the varieties of pleasures and pains than are animals. A being of higher faculties requires more to make him happy than does an animal, and suffering is greater for humans than for animals because humans are more complex psychologically. Some individuals have more refined tastes than others. So, said Mill, "Better to be a human being dissatisfied than a pig satisfied; better to be Socrates dissatisfied than a fool satisfied."

On this basis, then, how do we know what's right and what's wrong? As a utilitarian, Mill was committed to the view that *only consequences* matter. The rightness or wrongness of an act is determined by the goodness or badness of the results that follow. So we need to determine if a given decision results in more or less pleasure and pain. Human sensitivity to the varieties of pleasures and pains and human complexity in the experience of pleasure and pain surface a problem, however. With so many different qualities and quantities of pleasures and pains, how do we rank them? Mill's answer is that we should consult the experts—those who are completely familiar with both—that is, you and me! After all, humans themselves are the most sensitive to the varieties and complexities of pleasures and pains. We should rank pleasures and pains along multiple axes according to the experience of the majority of us.

Mill's principle of utility followed his consequentialist paradigm: "It is desirable, and in that sense right (or correct), to act so as to maximize the greatest happiness or minimize the greatest unhappiness, for the greatest number of persons." The decision that results in the greatest happiness for the greatest number of persons is the right decision. Mill defined happiness this way:

> Not a life of rapture, but moments of such, in an existence made up of few and temporary pains, many and various pleasures, with a decided predominance of the active over the passive, and having as the foundation of the whole, not expecting more out of life than it is capable of bestowing.

Happiness is the only thing desirable as an end in itself, according to Mill. It is the sole end of human action. How do we know? We know because people desire it.

When faced with a decision whether to tell a lie, Mill would have us ask, does telling the lie maximize the greatest happiness as measured in pleasures or maximize unhappiness? If the decision results in greater happiness over unhappiness, we have found the right action.

There are several commendable aspects to Mill's ethical theory. First, we are rightly concerned about consequences. We want our ethical decision to result in a better result. Second, pleasure and pain are clearly important factors in moral decision making. Generally speaking, we are risk averse and pleasure seeking. We should certainly avoid unnecessary pain. Finally, Mill's theory requires that we calculate the cost-and-benefit ratio of our behaviors.

Utilitarianism is also problematic in a number of ways. The theory seems to permit decisions that violate our reflective judgments. For instance, we know slavery is wrong. But on a utilitarian account, could someone justify keeping just a few slaves if he could show that many people would benefit? Utilitarianism also tends to treat one person's pleasure and pain as equivalent to another's. Yet we know that pain is idiosyncratic. Everyone has a distinct pain threshold physically, emotionally, spiritually, and in every other way. How could we measure hedons (units of pleasure or pain) accurately and scientifically, especially if they are unique to each person? Finally, when calculating happiness, how far into the future must one account for pleasure and pain? Many of our ethical decisions have to do with the impact of our behavior on future generations. In the area of environmental stewardship, for instance, one reason I am concerned about renewable energy sources is not so much for myself as for those who come after me. It is very likely that we will have enough gasoline for the remainder of our lives, but what about the lives of our grandchildren and great-grandchildren? Do we not owe it to them to be good stewards of our current resources? How do we calculate that? This is a significant problem for utilitarianism.

THE FAILURE OF THE ENLIGHTENMENT PROJECT

Kant, Bentham, Mill, and other Enlightenment thinkers tried to replace religion-based forms of morality with what they thought were reason-based forms. Because they set out to establish morality on the basis of human rationality, they thought they had achieved a new universal ethic. Instead, the result was essentially an impasse between Kantians and Mill's followers, between deontologists and utilitarians. The views turned out to be incommensurable, and there was no external position from which to adjudicate between them.

Louis Pojman (pronounced "Poyman," 1935–2005) offered a helpful critique of what he calls Action-Based Ethics (ABEs), such as deontology and utilitarianism. First, ABEs lack a motivational component. That is, although they attempt to answer the question, What is good?, they do not answer the question, Why should I want to do the good? "Action-based ethics are uninspiring, even boring—and largely negative. They fail to motivate or inspire to action. Ethics becomes a sort of mental plumbing, moral casuistry, a set of hairsplitting distinctions that somehow loses track of the purposes of morality altogether."[6] Why should I care either about duty or consequences for the greater number of persons? Why not be an egoist, someone who cares only about my own interests and well-being?

Second, ABEs are founded on a theological-legal model that is no longer appropriate, according to Pojman. ABEs tend to be legalistic. "Traditional, natural law ethics," he said, "used this model with integrity, for it saw more principles analogous to law and God

---

[6] Louis P. Pojman, *Ethics: Discovering Right and Wrong*, 5th ed. (Belmont, CA: Thomson Wadsworth, 2006), 157.

as analogous to the sovereign."[7] But the Enlightenment Project un-tethered ethics from its theological moorings. Furthermore, in a postmodern environment, legal theory is seen as pluralistic at best and relativistic at worst.

Third, ABEs often ignore the spiritual dimension of ethics, which includes gratitude, self-respect, sympathy, and compassion. These are moral terms, but they find no place in either Kantianism or in Mill's utilitarianism. The homicidal maniac who barely resists the temptation to murder, either because of duty or to reduce pain for others, turns out to be "the most glorious saint, surpassing the 'natural saint' who does good just because of a good character."[8]

Finally, Pojman says that ABEs overemphasize autonomy and neglect the communal context of ethics. We do not make moral decisions in a vacuum as lone, isolated, autonomous creatures. We are members of a moral community. In those communities loy-alty, sympathy, and shared concerns sustain the group. "In sum, rule-governed systems are uninspiring and unmotivating, negative, improperly legalistic, neglectful of the spiritual dimension, overly rationalistic, and atomistic."[9] Pojman says that all of this argues for a return to a virtue-based morality.

In his momentous volume *After Virtue*, Catholic philosopher Alasdair MacIntyre (b. 1929) argues that the Enlightenment Project not only happened to fail but *had* to fail.[10] The impasse between moral theories—including Kantian deontology and Mill's utili-tarianism—left us with a moral world that was essentially emotiv-ist, according to MacIntyre. Since it seems impossible to decide about a single moral theory on the basis of pure reason alone, we live in a world where the definition of the good is "I approve of

---

[7] Ibid., 158.
[8] Ibid., 159.
[9] Ibid., 160.
[10] On this point see Brad J. Kallenberg, "The Master Argument of MacIntyre's *After Virtue*," in *Virtues and Practices in the Christian Tradition: Christian Ethics After MacIntyre*, ed. Nancey Murphy, Brad J. Kallenberg, and Mark Thiessen Nation (Harrisburg, PA: Trinity Press International, 1997), 11.

this." Emotional response to right and wrong, good and bad, is the only measure of the good. In other words, people make ethical decisions on the basis of their personal preferences, attitudes, and feelings. And one person's preferences may not be another person's preferences. So we are left with intractable moral disputes and no objective means of resolving them. MacIntyre maintains that only by recovering Aristotelian virtue theory can we ultimately avoid another civil war.

✝ 5

EVANGELICAL ETHICS

Evangelical ethics is typically grounded in a Divine Command morality of one sort or another. In Divine Command ethics, reason plays a subsidiary role to special revelation. For evangelicals the scriptures of the Old and New Testaments are the *Norma norman non Normata* (the norm of norms that is not normed). That is to say, the Bible is the norming norm or revealed basis for evangelical reflection about the true, the good, and the beautiful. It is against the canon (rule) of Scripture that evangelicals seek to compare and contrast all moral teaching.

JOHN MURRAY

Divine Command ethics in the Reformed evangelical tradition is seen clearly with John Murray (1898–1975), who taught at Princeton Seminary. He was among the founders of Westminster Theological Seminary, where he taught systematic theology for over thirty years. His volume *Principles of Conduct* has been a mainstay in evangelical ethics for decades. Essentially an expanded collection of lectures Murray gave at Fuller Theological Seminary in 1955, *Principles of Conduct* is an excellent example of an evangelical methodology. "If ethics is concerned with manner of life and behavior," says Murray, "biblical ethics is concerned with the manner of life and behavior which the Bible requires and which the faith of the Bible produces."[1]

---

[1] John Murray, *Principles of Conduct: Aspects of Biblical Ethics* (Grand Rapids, MI: Eerdmans, 1957), 12.

By no means a comprehensive treatment of biblical ethics, *Principles of Conduct* covers some very important territory for evangelical reflection on the Bible's ethical teaching. Chapters include analyses of the creation ordinances, marriage and procreation, labor, the sanctity of life, the sanctity of truth, the Sermon on the Mount, law and grace, the dynamic of the biblical ethic, and the fear of God. In his chapter "The Dynamic of the Biblical Ethic," Murray said, "It is impossible to segregate the biblical ethic from the teaching of Scripture on other subjects. The ethic of the Bible reflects the character of the God of the Bible. Remove from Scripture the transcendent holiness, righteousness, and truth of God and its ethic disintegrates."[2]

In contrast to the natural-law tradition, Murray's understanding of the human condition makes it impossible for all individuals to conform to the holy God's moral requirements. Only those who experience union with Christ in salvation are able to embrace his principles of conduct, and even then, imperfectly.

> One feature of the witness of Scripture that bears directly upon the biblical ethic is its teaching on the depravity of human nature. "There is none righteous, no, not one. . . . There is none that doeth good, no, not even one" (Romans 3:10, 12). According to the Bible human depravity is such that the fulfillment of the demands of the biblical ethic is an impossibility. The mind of the flesh, the mind of the natural man, "is not subject to the law of God, neither indeed can it be" (Romans 8:7). It is this impossibility that makes necessary the provisions of redemptive grace.[3]

CARL F. H. HENRY

Standing as a pillar among his peers, another thinker who shaped evangelical theology and ethics was Carl F. H. Henry (1913–2003). Featured on the cover of *Time* magazine in 1977, Henry was called the leading theologian of American evangelicalism. Not only was

---

[2] Ibid., 202.
[3] Ibid.

he the founding editor of *Christianity Today*, but also he helped establish the National Association of Evangelicals, Fuller Theological Seminary, and the World Congress on Evangelism, which later became the Lausanne Congress. His magnum opus was his six-volume *God, Revelation and Authority*, published over a period of seven years.

Dedicated to his "Students in Ethics and Christian Ethics," his volume *Christian Personal Ethics* was published in 1957. Henry's knowledge of philosophy and theology was encyclopedic. Unlike Murray's volume, *Christian Personal Ethics* began with nearly 150 pages of analysis and critique of both secular and Christian ethics from the Sophists to Karl Barth and Emil Brunner. His engagement with Christian ethicists past and present was expansive. In one chapter he cites Archibald Alexander, an old Princeton theologian, and Paul Ramsey, a contemporary of Henry's from the Methodist tradition. In the same chapter he engages everyone from Calvin to A. B. Bruce to Jacques Maritain to H. Wheeler Robinson.

Like Murray, however, Henry maintained that

> the Hebrew-Christian ethic is transcendently revealed. Its source is a special Divine disclosure to man. In contrast with the ethics of human insight and speculative genius, Christian ethics is the ethic of revealed religion. In the preface to the Ten Commandments stands a dramatic and momentous phrase that is characteristic of revelational ethics: "And God spake all these words" (Exodus 20:1). From this source it gains an eternal and absolute quality. It communicates to man commands and norms that are unaffected by society or by time or by place.[4]

Writing on the threshold of the 1960s, Henry is well aware that "love is in the air" in every aspect of culture, including ethics. After all, liberal theologian Paul Tillich had said, "Love is the ultimate law," and in 1963 Joseph Fletcher would publish his dispropor-

---

[4] Carl F. H. Henry, *Christian Personal Ethics* (Grand Rapids, MI: Eerdmans, 1957), 188.

tionately popular *Situation Ethics* in which he argued that "the ruling norm of Christian decision is love: nothing else." For Henry, however, love was not amorphous or relativistic, but grounded in God's revelation:

> Love, as the Bible exposits it, is not something as nebulous as moderns would have us think. The New Testament knows nothing of lawless believers in Christ. No believer is left to work out his moral solutions by the principle of love alone. He has some external guidance from Divine revelation. The early believers were not delivered from an obligation to obey the precepts of the law. The life of love which Christianity proclaims is centered in love for the Living God who has revealed his will, and only to the extent that love impels the believer to fulfill God's revealed will is genuinely of the Holy Spirit. Love is in accord with the biblical ethic when it devotedly seeks to obey fully the Divine commands.
>
> The content of love must be defined by Divine revelation. The biblical revelation places the only reliable rule of practice before the community of faith. What the Bible teaches gives trustworthy direction to love of self, of neighbor, of God. The pages of the Bible are filled with an interest in good fathers and children, good husbands and wives, good neighbors and friends, good rulers and subjects, good states and the good life, and the feeling of love even in the regenerate believer is inadequate to chart the whole implication of the moral life.[5]

Henry also published a much smaller volume, *Aspects of Christian Social Ethics*, in 1964. In one sense, this volume was partial payment on a promissory note he issued in his 1947 manifesto, *The Uneasy Conscience of Modern Fundamentalism*. In *Uneasy Conscience*, Henry called for evangelical renewal, cultural engagement, and social transformation. In *Aspects of Christian Social Ethics*, he raised questions that remain with us today: "How much shall we trust *legislation* and how much shall we trust *regeneration* to change the social setting? What should we expect the *State* to

---

[5] Ibid., 255.

contribute, what should we expect the *Church* to contribute, if we are seeking a society ruled by justice and love."[6]

From personal conversations with Dr. Henry, I know he saw his work in social ethics as an unfinished project. He continued to hope that someone would complete a more comprehensive evangelical social ethic during his lifetime. No one did. His conclusion to *Aspects of Christian Social Ethics* is as breathtaking today as it must have been in the 1960s.

> The Christian Church does not initiate movements for political independence. "My kingdom does not belong to this world," said Jesus (John 18:36 NEB). Yet Christianity is not ashamed or apologetic, as if on that account it merely laps up the privileges others have earned. For the Church remains ready to proclaim and ready to be martyred for proclaiming those abiding truths and ultimate loyalties whose surrender reduces every revolution to lawlessness and whose loss casts even a free people into subjection and nihilism.[7]

ARTHUR F. HOLMES

Tens, perhaps hundreds of thousands, of evangelical Christian college students will be familiar with the name Arthur Holmes (1924–2011). Holmes taught philosophy at Wheaton College for forty-three years and produced an enormous body of work, including his benchmark volume, *All Truth Is God's Truth*, in 1977. He was one of the founders of the Society of Christian Philosophers, thought deeply about Christian higher education, and was greatly revered for his contribution to Christian intellectual reflection. His volumes have been used in philosophy and ethics courses in North American colleges and beyond. By 2007 his volume *Ethics: Approaches to Moral Decisions* in the Contours of Christian Philosophy series, originally published in 1984, had already sold over sixty thousand copies.

---

[6] Carl F. H. Henry, *Aspects of Christian Social Ethics* (Grand Rapids, MI: Eerdmans, 1964), 15, emphasis original.
[7] Ibid., 186.

Ethics was written against the backdrop of the 1960s revolution as a way of introducing Christians to both ethical theory and application. Holmes saw ethics as more related to religion than to the social sciences. He also understood the Judeo-Christian tradition as one of the main historical forces behind the moral heritage of the West. Thoroughly familiar with the history of both Western and non-Western philosophy, Holmes put a Christian ethical perspective in conversation with other approaches.

Although he was committed to the authority of the Bible, Holmes saw the importance of Christian ethical reflection, because "Christians do not claim that the Bible is exhaustive, that it tells us everything we can know or can benefit ethically from knowing. It is silent about many things, including many of the moral problems we face today—problems in bio- and medical ethics, for example, problems about responsibility to unborn generations and about population control."[8]

Happiness could not be the definition of the good for Holmes. Since, in the words of the Westminster Shorter Catechism, "our highest end is to glorify and enjoy God forever (*not* to enjoy *ourselves* as much as we can),"[9] love for God must take priority over other ends. For Holmes, God's love and justice are defining attributes for Christian morality. Loving God, therefore, includes doing what God wills as we work out the implications of his love and justice in a fallen world. But, he acknowledged, "there is more to morality than doing what is right."[10] Because motives and intentions are also important, Christian virtues and character are vital to a distinctly Christian ethic. Thus, "moral formation is naturally connected to faith development, and devotion to God as the Good gives purpose to one's whole life. That is what the distinctive practices of the Christian tradition are essentially about: a love for God

---

[8] Arthur F. Holmes, *Ethics: Approaches to Moral Decisions*, 2nd ed. (Downers Grove, IL: InterVarsity, 2007), 14.
[9] Ibid., 52.
[10] Ibid., 131.

that pays close attention to the Scriptures and prayer and the sacraments of the church."[11] A shared vision of the good, in Holmes's view, underwrites the formative practices of the church.

STANLEY HAUERWAS

Among Anabaptists and Methodists, perhaps no ethicist has been more influential in the late twentieth and early twenty-first centuries than Stanley Hauerwas (b. 1940). In 2001 he was named "best theologian in America" by *Time* magazine. When informed of this award, he remarked in his own inimical way, "'Best' is not a theological category."[12]

A prolific writer, colorful speaker, popular professor, and lover of laughter, Hauerwas has shaped an entire generation of graduate students at the University of Notre Dame and, since 1984, at Duke University, directing over fifty dissertations. Having written his own dissertation at Yale, titled "Character and the Christian Life," Hauerwas has remained deeply committed to a virtue ethic with enormous ecclesial implications. He has written eloquently on pacifism, community, and responsibility for persons with disabilities, among other moral concerns.

In *The Peaceable Kingdom: A Primer in Christian Ethics*, Hauerwas argues that "the nature of Christian ethics is determined by the fact that Christian convictions take the form of a story, or perhaps better, a set of stories that constitutes a tradition, which in turn creates and forms a community."[13] Christianity is first and foremost a narrative that describes God's dealing with creation, humanity, and his church. This story, according to Hauerwas, reminds us that our existence and that of the world is contingent on God. Second, the story situates us historically within a community where the self is both discovered through and subordinate to the

---

[11] Ibid., 140.
[12] Stanley Hauerwas, *Hannah's Child: A Theologian's Memoir* (Grand Rapids, MI: Eerdmans, 2010), *ix*.
[13] Stanley Hauerwas, *The Peaceable Kingdom: A Primer in Christian Ethics* (Notre Dame, IN: University of Notre Dame Press, 1983), 24.

community. Third, God has revealed himself within a narrative, namely, in the history of Israel and in the life of Jesus. "Christian ethics, therefore, is not first of all concerned," says Hauwerwas, "with 'Thou shalt' or 'Thou shalt not.' Its first task is to help us rightly envision the world. Christian ethics is specifically formed by a very definite story with determinative content."[14]

The Christian story, says Hauerwas, teaches us to be a sinner. That is, it shows us that we are not guilty of petty crimes but treason against the Almighty. Not only so, but we deceive ourselves about reality. So the Christian story tells of a God who exposes our sinfulness and invites us to place ourselves in his history. "Redemption . . . is a change in which we accept the invitation to become part of God's kingdom, a kingdom through which we acquire a character befitting one who has heard God's call."[15]

For Hauerwas the task of Christian ethics is the task of being the church. As a story-formed community, the church is separate from the larger society and should seek to live its story as consistently as possible. The politics of the kingdom of God is radically different from the politics of the world. The church is characterized by three New Testament realities: forgiveness, the cross, and the resurrection. "Through Jesus' resurrection we see God's peace as a present reality."[16] For Hauerwas, God's peace enables us to be peace loving, hospitable, and charitable. Christians not only should be "militant pacifists," but also should be committed to the protection of life as an eschatological commitment. "We do not value life as an end in itself—there is much worth dying for—rather all life is valued, even as the lives of our enemies, because God has valued them."[17]

In an essay published in the *South Atlantic Quarterly* against the backdrop of September 11, 2001, Hauerwas sums up his pacifism nicely:

---

[14] Ibid., 27.
[15] Ibid., 33.
[16] Ibid., 88.
[17] Ibid., 90.

Christians are not called to be heroes or shoppers. We are called to be holy. We do not think holiness is an individual achievement, but rather a set of practices to sustain a people who refuse to have their lives determined by the fear and denial of death. We believe by so living we offer our non-Christian brothers and sisters an alternative to all politics based on the denial of death. Christians are acutely aware that we seldom are faithful to the gifts God has given us, but we hope the confession of our sins is a sign of hope in a world without hope. This means pacifists do have a response to September 11, 2001. Our response is to continue living in a manner that witnesses to our belief that the world was not changed on September 11, 2001. The world was changed during the celebration of Passover in A.D. 33.[18]

OLIVER O'DONOVAN

Oliver O'Donovan (b. 1945) is probably the leading theological ethicist working in the United Kingdom. An Anglican, he is currently the professor of Christian ethics and practical theology at the School of Divinity, New College, Edinburgh, a position that he has held since the summer of 2006. He was Regius Professor of Moral and Pastoral Theology and Canon of Christ Church at the University of Oxford in England from 1982 to 2006. Like Hauerwas, he has supervised many North American and British doctoral students who are now in professorships around the world.

One contemporary has called O'Donovan's trilogy, *Resurrection and the Moral Order, The Desire of Nations,* and *The Ways of Judgement,* "the most accomplished contribution to Anglican ethics since World War II."[19] His ministry continues to have a tremendous impact on evangelicals and others worldwide.

Most of O'Donovan's recent work has been devoted to proposing a "natural ethic" different from a Catholic natural-law ethic. *Resurrection and the Moral Order* begins with this declaration:

---

[18] Stanley Hauerwas, "September 11, 2001: A Pacifist Response," *South Atlantic Quarterly* 101 (Spring 2002), http://today.duke.edu/showcase/mmedia/features/911site/hauerwas.html.

[19] Samuel Wells, ed., *Christian Ethics: An Introductory Reader* (Malden, MA: John Wiley, 2010), 13.

"The foundations of Christian ethics must be evangelical foundations; or, to put it more simply, Christian ethics must arise from
the gospel of Jesus Christ. Otherwise, it could not be Christian
ethics."[20] Easter morning restored and fulfilled the moral order of
creation and, as importantly, liberates us to make ethical choices.
O'Donovan's approach is teleological and, therefore, eschatological since that is the final aim of all things. Through redemption
God is directing creation toward its destiny in the exalted Christ.

The upshot of his approach is seen in this pregnant paragraph:

> Each area has to be given, as it were, a salvation-history of its
> own. Marriage is a gift of creation; it is taken into the reconciling
> fellowship of Christ; it is confronted with the challenge of the
> eschatological kingdom. Telling the truth is a task entrusted to
> Adam as he names the animals; it is a responsibility of redeemed
> humankind which has been told the truth about itself in Jesus;
> and the full disclosure of the truth is the content of God's future
> judgment. Work is a gift of creation; it is ennobled into mutual
> service in the fellowship of Christ; it gives place to the final sab-
> bath rest. And so on.[21]

So God is not in the business of restoring creation to some pristine
condition before the fall. The garden of Eden is not the destination.
Rather, everything is moving toward the hope of a new heaven and
a new earth, which was promised through Christ. We currently
live with an eschatological tension. Although the created order has
been vindicated by the resurrection of Jesus from the dead, it is not
yet fully redeemed.

O'Donovan's work in political philosophy is largely the out-
working of the implications of Christ's resurrection for living in this
late-modern period. The church is a "post-political" community,
a fellowship that is "authorized by the ascended Christ."[22] So the

[20] Oliver O'Donovan, *Resurrection and the Moral Order: An Outline for Evangelical Ethics*, 2nd ed.
(Grand Rapids, MI: Eerdmans, 1994), 11.
[21] Ibid., *vxvii*.
[22] Oliver O'Donovan, *The Ways of Judgment* (Grand Rapids, MI: Eerdmans, 2008), 240.

church has its own authority and is not answerable to any human authority that may attempt to subsume it. Indeed, the church is a community that demonstrates and bears witness to how life should be lived as it is drawn toward its destiny in the risen Christ.

GILBERT MEILAENDER

A Lutheran theologian, Gilbert Meilaender (b. 1946) is the Richard and Phyllis Duesenberg Professor of Christian Ethics at Valparaiso University. He has served on the editorial board and as an associate editor of the *Journal of Religious Ethics*, as an associate editor for *Religious Studies Review*, on the editorial board of the *Annual of the Society of Christian Ethics*, and on the editorial advisory board of *First Things*. He has written in many areas of ethics including work, friendship, virtue theory, and the social and ethical thought of C. S. Lewis. A student of the late Paul Ramsey, much of Meilaender's attention has focused on issues in bioethics. His book *Bioethics: A Primer for Christians* has become a standard introductory guide to the subject. Meilaender served with excellence as a member of the President's Council on Bioethics under the Bush administration from its inception in 2002.

In *Neither Beast Nor God: The Dignity of the Human Person*, Meilaender defends the notion of human dignity against the acids of late modernity. For instance, Steven Pinker, the atheistic professor of cognitive science, infamously critiqued the President's Council on Bioethics for its work on human dignity in his essay "The Stupidity of Dignity" in the liberal magazine *The New Republic*. With the wisdom of a seasoned theologian, Meilaender winsomely and courageously expounds the dignity of the human person made in the image of God. He separates for examination both human dignity and personal dignity. Human dignity "has to do with the powers and limits characteristic of our species," while personal dignity "has to do not with species-specific powers and limits but with the individual person, whose dignity calls for our respect whatever his or her powers and limits may be."[23] His volume concludes:

> The dignity of our humanity and the dignity of our person thus coinhere. We know persons only as bodies, and when we encounter a living human body our moral task is to seek to recognize the person who is there. I doubt that anyone can simply be compelled into such recognition by rational argument alone. The heart must be open to recognize personal dignity in every living human being (even those who are far from flourishing in the ways that characterize the dignity of the human species). We must be ready to set aside the notion that we should evaluate their claim to personal dignity and accept the truth that, in our willingness or unwillingness to acknowledge it, we judge ourselves.[24]

There are doubtless other Christian and evangelical ethicists who deserve mention. Some of them will be members of the Society of Christian Ethics in America, or the Society for the Study of Christian Ethics in the United Kingdom. But even more of them work in classrooms, think tanks, public policy, and businesses around the world.

---

[23] Gilbert Meilaender, *Neither Beast Nor God: The Dignity of the Human Person* (New York: New Atlantis, 2009), 8.
[24] Ibid., 103–4.

6

USING THE BIBLE IN MORAL DECISION MAKING

How do we move from the ancient text of the Bible to contemporary ethical issues? How can we apply the witness of the Old and New Testaments to cutting-edge ethical issues in medicine, politics, science, and public policy? The short answer is that, as the apostle Peter told the faithful Christians in Asia Minor, "[God's] divine power has granted to us all things that pertain to life and godliness, through the knowledge of him who called us to his own glory and excellence" (2 Pet. 1:3a). In other words, God has not left his people without guidance in every area of life. Although the Bible is not a science textbook, its message speaks to the deep underlying values that can guide decisions about scientific matters. Although the Bible is not a manual of medicine, its truths may be applied to medical decision making. Although the Bible is not a policy manual, its principles may inform how we think about government and politics. Christians have understood the role of the Bible in ethics in a number of ways. Here are a few of the most prevalent views.

THE BIBLE AS LAW CODE

Some Christians understand the Bible to be a book of eternal laws. They argue that if people want to know what to do, they should consult the commandments and ordinances of the Old and New Testaments. Paying attention to the laws and rules of the Bible is the way to discern moral right and wrong. Interestingly, this strategy often turns out to be a popular Christian version of the way the Jewish rabbis understood the Old Testament. The ancient rabbis taught that the Torah (the first five books of the Old Testament) could be summarized in 613 commandments or *mitzvot*. Living ethically meant keeping all 613 laws. Some Christians treat the commandments, the teachings of Jesus, the prescriptions of Paul, or all three the same way the rabbis treated the *mitzvot*. Find a rule and follow it.

The problem with this method of applying Scripture is, first, that the Bible is much more than a book of rules. The sixty-six books of the Old and New Testaments do, indeed, include commandments and precepts. They also include historical, wisdom, and prophetic literature. There are songs, poems, and letters. If Christians are to take seriously the entire body of God's revelation in the Bible, they must take seriously the variety of ways and times in which God has revealed his will.

THE BIBLE AS UNIVERSAL PRINCIPLES

Another way some Christians approach the biblical material is to view it as a source of principles to be discerned for ethical decision making. This view acknowledges that the Old and New Testaments are historically situated and cannot always translate easily into a contemporary context. So, rather than look for specific commandments, these Christians attempt to discern the underlying principles that they believe inform those commandments.

For instance, the Old Testament tells God's people not to mix different types of fabric (Lev. 19:19) or round off the hair on their temples (Lev. 19:27). Why do Christians routinely violate both of these statutes? These texts are part of the Holiness Code (Leviticus 17–26), a section of Leviticus that emphasizes both the holiness of God and the way his people are to be holy and set apart from the pagan nations around them. Christians do not understand these commands to be applied literally today, but they do believe the underlying principle applies, namely, that God's people are to be holy and set apart from the pagan culture around them. Christians are to be identifiable as God's own people in their behavior and practices.

Seeing the Bible as only a book of universal principles is also fraught with difficulties. First, as with the Bible-as-law-code view, this perspective does not take into account the rich diversity of biblical teaching about ethics. In some cases in the Bible, we are given persons to imitate rather than principles to apply. The Beatitudes Jesus taught in the Sermon on the Mount (Matt. 5:3–10), for instance, are not principles to be followed but virtues to be lived and cultivated. Seeing the Bible only as principles also deprives us of what is found in the Wisdom Literature. Books such as Psalms, Proverbs, and Ecclesiastes are suffused with great wisdom, much of which is in the form of stories, examples, and illustrations, not principles. Second, because the task of identifying the principles depends on our discernment, we must be very careful that we have perceived and applied them correctly. This is not always easily done.

THE BIBLE AS COMMUNITY NARRATIVE

Some scholars emphasize the Bible as a grand narrative, a sacred story of God's redemptive acts among his people. Living faithfully, they argue, means situating oneself in the story and living accordingly. The people of God—the church—are to see themselves as participants in this grand narrative. This view helpfully points out that the thirty-nine books of the Old Testament and the twenty-seven books of the New Testament, despite their various genres, contexts, and time periods, form a cohesive drama with leading characters, heroes and villains, plots and twists, morals and lessons, and a climactic ending. In fact, one of the evidences of divine authorship of the Bible is the way it coheres from Genesis to Revelation, despite the number of authors and number of years separating the various books of Scripture.

But the Bible is not only narrative. Some of the Bible is didactic, some is poetic, and some is epistolary. Scripture includes timeless rules such as the Ten Commandments, and robust principles such as the principle of holiness. The problem with understanding the Bible as merely a story, however, is that one may be tempted to neglect those timeless rules and enduring principles.

THE BIBLE AS CANONICAL REVELATION OF DIVINE COMMANDS, PRINCIPLES, AND CHRISTIAN VIRTUES

The Bible should be understood, I would argue, as a canonical revelation of God's commands, principles, and virtues. First, it is canonical. That is to say, the Bible is the book of the church. The books included in the canon (meaning "rule" or "measuring stick") were recognized by the church as divinely inspired and authoritative. Those books are the church's only rule of faith and practice.

Second, the Bible is God's revelation. God has made himself and his will known in the person of Christ and in the scriptures of the Old and New Testaments. As Paul said to the young pastor Timothy, "All Scripture is breathed out by God and profitable for teaching, for reproof, for correction, and for training in righteousness, that the man of God may be complete, equipped for every good work" (2 Tim. 3:16–17). The church has confessed that God's revelation is a sufficient guide for knowing his will. Furthermore, the books of the Bible reflect various types of literature, including history, poetry, wisdom, prophecy, apocalyptic, and letters. Accurate interpretation and proper application require that readers attend to the type of literature, the historical context, and the aim of each of those texts.

Third, God's moral instruction comes to us in the form of commands and principles and is also revealed in Christian virtues and examples. No one can deny (or should) that the Bible contains rules or commands. The Ten Commandments, for instance, stand as a lasting testimony to God's will for human flourishing. Likewise, enduring principles can be derived from the biblical witness. Even though, for instance, the Bible does not include a direct commandment forbidding the use of human beings as experimental guinea pigs against their wills, the principle of human dignity, grounded in the image of God, applies. Because we are made in the image of God, research should not be done on human subjects without consent. And because people are made in God's image, some research should not be done even with consent, because it would violate one's personhood.

Furthermore, not only does the Bible contain eternal commandments and universal principles; it also contains biographies of virtuous individuals—most notably Jesus of Nazareth—and descriptions of virtues to be cultivated by his followers. God has revealed himself in Jesus Christ, the Word made flesh (John 1). In the person of Christ we see the epitome of a virtuous human being. As both fully divine and fully human, Jesus is our exemplar. Likewise, Jesus's own teaching includes commands, principles, and virtues. As we have said, the Sermon on the Mount (Matthew 5–7) begins with a list of beatitudes or descriptions of the happily virtuous Christian. Poverty of spirit, mournfulness, meekness, hungering for righteousness, etc. (Matt. 5:3–12), are not rules to be followed but virtues to be inhabited. Much of the remainder of the sermon includes commands against anger, lust, divorce, taking oaths, and retaliation. Positively, Jesus commands his disciples to love their enemies, give to those in need, pray single-heartedly, fast, and store up treasures in heaven rather than on earth.

In addition to Jesus's example and instruction, the apostle Paul provides several lists of virtues that are to mark the Christian. Faith, hope, and love (1 Cor. 13:13) combine to make up the so-called theological virtues. Among other virtues are the fruit of the Spirit, those virtues that the Holy Spirit cultivates in the believer's life: "The fruit of the Spirit is love, joy, peace, patience, kindness, goodness, faithfulness, gentleness, self-control; against such things there is no law. And those who belong to Christ Jesus have crucified the flesh with its passions and desires" (Gal. 5:22–24). They describe the character of the faithful Christian and are to be operative in our decision making. And in more than one place Paul enjoins other Christians to be "imitators of me" (1 Cor. 4:16; 11:1) even as he is an imitator of God in Christ (1 Cor. 11:1; Eph. 5:1).

In his very helpful volume *Exploring Christian Ethics: Biblical Foundations for Morality*, Kyle Fedler offers some helpful guidelines about how to use Scripture. First, he says, realize that no single method for the use of Scripture is adequate. "The very diversity of the Bible itself warns us against a simplistic use." Interpret stories as story, history as history, epistles as epistles, and poetry as poetry.

Second, whenever possible Scripture should be read in its historical and cultural context. The first question we should ask of a given text is, What did the original readers and hearers understand the text to mean? This means we will need to situate ourselves as much as possible in the historical-cultural context of those original hearers. Knowing certain features of the history, geography, and climate of the ancient Near East may be helpful in understanding some texts. The biblical languages (Hebrew in the Old Testament and Greek and Aramaic in the New Testament) will often yield important insights about the way words were used. Archaeological discoveries may open up the meaning of certain passages of the Bible.

Third, Fedler reminds us that not all Scripture carries the same normative weight. For instance, some commands under the old covenant must be reinterpreted in light of the new covenant. The Old Testament prescriptions about animal sacrifice have all found their fulfillment in the sacrifice of Jesus, the Lamb of God. Although *principles* of the Holiness Code in Leviticus may be morally obligatory today, the *letter of the law* is not. In other words, we cannot "proof-text" to find answers to our moral questions. We cannot lift a Bible verse out of its literary, historical, and cultural context and expect to find help in decision making. This leads to a flat reading of Scripture.

Finally, although Scripture is primary, normative, and authoritative, it is not our only source of guidance and wisdom. Tradition—the way the church has dealt with similar cases in the past—may illuminate our understanding of the present. Experience will obviously be important in understanding the truth of the matter. And while we must not rely on human wisdom alone, the faculty of reason often helps to provide clarity about the moral questions of a case and can help us determine an appropriate course of action.

So the Bible has much to offer believers as they seek to obey the Lord in every area of life, but it is not always as easy as matching one Bible verse with a problem. After all, there are no biblical texts that speak directly to questions about human cloning or embryonic stem cell research or artificial intelligence. Careful attention must be paid, then, to discern the commands, principles, and virtues that apply in a particular context.

Below is a suggested procedure for finding ethical guidance from the Bible:

- Pray for divine illumination.
- Define the ethical issues or problems.
- Clarify the issue to be examined.
- Glean all scriptural data on the issue with attention to:
  - Commandments
  - Principles
  - Examples.
- Study the scriptural instruction carefully with attention to:
  - Genre
  - Literary style and organization
  - Definitions and grammar
  - Context
  - Overall theme, purpose, historical significance.

- What does the text say in its context?
- What does the text mean today?
- Apply the biblical instruction:
  - Engage in dialogue with the community of the faithful.
  - Study the history of Christian ethics.
- Formulate a Christian ethical position.

CONCLUSION

In sum, despite popular book titles, there are no such things as moral machines[1] or virtuous robots.[2] Ethics and morality are the unique domain of persons: divine, angelic, and human.

The good for human beings is to pursue their natural *telos*, aim, or purpose toward human flourishing. That end is ultimately eschatological, only fully realized in the life to come. In the meantime, in pursuit of human flourishing we constantly strive to reorder our loves in the face of our finitude and obstinacy and, at the same time, in the face of a world and systems that often conspire against our flourishing. So the pursuit of the good, the true, and the beautiful is difficult, to say the least.

Developing certain dispositions, practices, or virtues helps us achieve our end. The Bible points us to that end through its stories, commands, principles, and examples, and especially through the ministry of our exemplar, Jesus of Nazareth, the Son of the living God. Although every person may pursue the human *telos*, Christians enjoy the aid of the indwelling presence of the Holy Spirit, who motivates them both to will and to do God's good pleasure as they follow the path of the Lord Jesus.

Being human situates one in a distinct moral community of persons. Human flourishing is not possible apart from the human community, in part because a well-ordered life is not solipsistic, but one in which the provision and receipt of neighbor love is crucial. Love and friendship help us become who we are meant to be through Christ.

---

[1] Wendell Wallach, *Moral Machines: Teaching Robots Right from Wrong* (New York: Oxford University Press, 2010).

[2] Peter Danielson, *Artificial Morality: Virtuous Robots for Virtual Games* (New York: Routledge, 1992).

Decisions about social policy and government should be made in light of the end of the human person. The best policies serve the end of helping human beings to flourish individually and in community.

The most urgent question facing us today, then, is, What does it mean to be truly human? That question must be answered as we consider beginning-of-life ethics. Is an unborn human being deserving of our respect and protection as a member of our moral community? We struggle with this question at the end of life. Should we remove from life support someone who has lost her mental capacities? Is being human only about what is going on in the head? In between, the answer to the question invokes our loves and guides our reflection. How do I best love my neighbor in response to the love of God in Christ? In what ways can I contribute to his or her flourishing? What does neighbor love look like in business, politics, and education? These are profound moral questions. Nothing less than a truly human future depends upon those answers.

APPENDIX

REPRESENTATIVE DEFINITIONS OF CHRISTIAN ETHICS

Christian ethics . . . is defined as a systematic explanation of the moral example and teaching of Jesus applied to the total life of the individual in society and actualized by the power of the Holy Spirit. (Henlee Barnette, *Introducing Christian Ethics* [Nashville: B&H Academic, 1998], 3)

Christian ethics may be defined as critical reflection on the moral decisions and actions of individual Christians and of the Christian community. (Thomas Bufford Maston, *Why Live the Christian Life?* [Sevierville, TN: Insight, 1996], 11)

Using biblical-theological bases in association with the natural and social sciences and insights from philosophy, the fine arts, and humanities, Christian ethics is the study and application of the Christian faith in the individual and corporate dimensions of daily life. (William M. Tillman Jr. and Timothy D. Gilbert, *Christian Ethics: A Primer* [Nashville: Sunday School Publishing Board, 1986], 13)

All normative ethics attempts to identify the characteristics of a life worth living, and all examines and articulates standards to inform and guide us in shaping our actions and character. Christian ethics undertakes the same task with reference to Jesus of Nazareth. (Wayne G. Boulton, Thomas D. Kennedy, and Allen Verhey, *From Christ to the World: Introductory Readings in Christian Ethics* [Grand Rapids, MI: Eerdmans, 1994], 3)

In the New Testament, ethics follows from what membership in the kingdom demands. Ethics and discipleship overlap significantly. Little distinction is made between the moral and spiritual life, except that the former deals mainly with the believer's responsibility to the church and the world, while the latter relates to one's worship of God. A consistent pattern emerges in the New Testament in that Jesus and the apostles would initially preach the message of the kingdom, and then its ethical implications. But the ethical implications are addressed quickly, since it was inconceivable to the early church that someone would profess Christ and not adhere to the moral demands of life in the kingdom. (Scott Rae, *Moral Choices: An Introduction to Ethics* [Grand Rapids, MI: Zondervan, 2009], 29)

At the risk of oversimplification, the Christian universe consists of three components: God, the created world, and human beings. Faith claims about each of these contribute to the overall Christian emphasis on morality and ethics. Put differently, it is what Christians profess to believe about God, human beings, and the created world that makes ethics so central to Christianity. (Kyle D. Fedler, *Exploring Christian Ethics: Biblical Foundations for Morality* [Louisville, KY: Westminster, 2006], 9)

Morality is, then, about human flourishing and we need some rational principle to guide our decision-making about the kind of person we should be. We need to understand better the basis for the distinction between right and wrong, good and evil. We need to understand, in other words, what the word "moral" actually means. By its very nature, therefore, ethics is practical. This may seem an obvious point: after all, ethics involves reflection about human conduct. (Alban McCoy, *An Intelligent Person's Guide to Christian Ethics* [New York: Bloomsbury Academic, 2006], 13)

Christian ethics is methodological reflection on the values, norms, virtues, and purposes of Christian life in one's contemporary context, drawing on Scripture and the tradition of faith. (Patrick Nullens and Ronald T. Michener, *The Matrix of Christian Ethics: Integrating Philosophy and Moral Theology in a Postmodern Context* [Downers Grove, IL: InterVarsity, 2010], 12)

A discipline of thought and action that spells out the practical import of Christian convictions on daily life. It makes concrete how our theological beliefs about humanity, the world, and God can help us to be the kind of people who are committed to following Jesus. (Harry J. Huebner, *An Introduction to Christian Ethics: History, Movements, People* [Waco, TX: Baylor University Press, 2012], 4)

QUESTIONS FOR REFLECTION

1. How frequently has the relativist claim that there is no universal truth about right and wrong been used as a conversation stopper? What strategies can you think of that will move the discussion along?

2. What is the contribution of the Judeo-Christian tradition to the morality of Western civilization? How have examples such as the Good Samaritan and the Golden Rule shaped traditional morality?

3. What do you understand to be the relationship between the ethical requirements of the Old Testament and the New Testament? What parts of the Old Testament moral code are still valid for today? Why?

4. Faith, hope, and love are regarded as the chief Christian virtues. How do those virtues shape the ethical decision making of the Christian? How does the fruit of the Spirit (Gal. 5:22–24) shape one's moral choices?

5. Why isn't reason a sufficient foundation for ethics? Why did the Enlightenment Project fail to provide universal ethical agreement? What is the role of revelation, reason, tradition, and personal experience in your own decision-making procedure?

6. How does the Christian community, including the church, influence your ethical behavior? How can you encourage your Christian friends and family to be more faithful morally?

TIMELINE

16th–12th century BC	Ten Commandments
563–483 BC	Buddha
551–479 BC	Confucius
469–399 BC	Socrates
429–347 BC	Plato
c. 350 BC	Aristotle, *Nicomachean Ethics*
322 BC	Stoic school founded
7–5 BC—AD 30–36	Jesus of Nazareth
c. 85–110	*Didache; Teaching of the Twelve Apostles*
133–190	Athenagoras of Athens
354–430	St. Augustine
480–547	St. Benedict
1225–1274	St. Thomas Aquinas
1483–1546	Martin Luther
1509–1564	John Calvin
1642–1651	Thomas Hobbes, *Leviathan*
1724–1804	Immanuel Kant
1748–1832	Jeremy Bentham
1759–1833	William Wilberforce
1806–1873	John Stuart Mill
1873–1958	G. E. Moore
1884–1972	Harry S. Truman
1887–1948	Ruth Benedict
1898–1963	C. S. Lewis
1898–1975	John Murray
1907–1972	Abraham Joshua Heschel
1913–2003	Carl F. H. Henry
1917–1981	J. L. Mackie
1920–2010	Philippa Foot

1924–2011	Arthur F. Holmes
1926–2006	Clifford Geertz
1929–	Alasdair MacIntyre
1935–2005	Louis Pojman
1940–	Stanley Hauerwas
1945–	Oliver O'Donovan
1946–	Gilbert Meilaender
1946–	Peter Singer
1960–	Christian Smith

GLOSSARY

applied ethics. The practical application of one's normative ethical theory to any variety of areas such as business, medicine, military, and society.

axiology. The study of value, whether ethical value, aesthetic value, economic value, or other ways of studying the worth of something.

consequentialism. Any ethical theory that focuses on the outcomes or consequences of ethical choices rather than on rules, principles, or virtues.

cultural relativism. The view that one's culture determines what is right and what is wrong and that there are no universal, cross-cultural moral norms.

deontology. *Deon* is from the Greek meaning "rule" or "duty." Deontological ethics are rule-based ethics. See also *principlism*.

descriptive ethics. The study of a person's or group's moral thought or behavior. This way of studying ethics offers no evaluation or assessment of the rightness or wrongness of a particular behavior or way of thinking but merely describes the moral state of affairs.

Divine Command ethics. An ethical theory in which the definition of the morally good is that which is equivalent to God's will.

ethical egoism. The view that moral good and bad are defined by the individual and his or her self-interest alone.

ethical hedonism. The idea that "the good" is defined by pleasure. Pleasure is good; pain is bad.

metaethics. The study of what is meant by ethical terms such as *good*, *bad*, *right*, and *wrong*.

normative ethical relativism. The idea that relativism should be normative or the way things ought to be.

normative ethics. A theory of morality that prescribes a certain way of thinking about ethical questions or gives an account of what makes certain behaviors obligatory.

prescriptive ethics. See *normative ethics*.

principlism. Another name for a rule-based or deontological ethical theory.

relativism. The view that right and wrong, good and bad, and other moral notions are not objective, universal, and absolute but vary according to time, location, or situation.

shalom. Hebrew word meaning "completeness," "wholeness," or "overall welfare."

utilitarianism. A form of consequentialism in which the right action is that which maximizes the greatest happiness for the greatest number of persons or sentient beings.

virtue theory. A theory of right and wrong that focuses on the kind of person one should be morally rather than on the kind of action one should perform.

RESOURCES FOR FURTHER STUDY

Boulton, Wayne G., Thomas D. Kennedy, and Allen Verhey. *From Christ to the World: Introductory Readings in Christian Ethics*. Grand Rapids, MI: Baker, 1994.

Clark, David K., and Robert V. Rakestraw. *Readings in Christian Ethics*. Vol. 1 of *Theory and Method*. Grand Rapids, MI: Baker, 1994.

_____. *Readings In Christian Ethics*. Vol. 2 of *Issues and Applications*. Grand Rapids, MI: Baker, 1996.

Davis. John Jefferson. *Evangelical Ethics: Issues Facing the Church Today*. Phillipsburg, NJ: P&R, 2004.

Eckman, James P. *Biblical Ethics: Choosing Right in a World Gone Wrong*. Wheaton, IL: Crossway, 2004.

Feinberg, John S., and Paul D. Feinberg. *Ethics for a Brave New World*. 2nd ed. Wheaton, IL: Crossway, 1993.

Grenz, Stanley J. *The Moral Quest: Foundations of Christian Ethics*. Downers Grove, IL: InterVarsity, 1997.

Gushee, David P., and Glen H. Stassen. *Kingdom Ethics: Following Jesus in Contemporary Context*. Downers Grove, IL: IVP Academic, 2003.

Hays, Richard B. *The Moral Vision of the New Testament: Community, Cross, New Creation: A Contemporary Introduction to New Testament Ethics*. New York: HarperOne, 1996.

Heubner, Harry J. *An Introduction to Christian Ethics: History, Movements, People*. Waco, TX: Baylor University Press, 2012.

Hill, Michael. *The How and Why of Love: An Introduction to Evangelical Ethics*. Kingsford, Australia: Matthias Press, 2002.

Hollinger, Dennis P. *Choosing the Good: Christian Ethics in a Complex World*. Grand Rapids, MI: Baker Academic, 2002.

Kaiser, Walter C. *What Does the Lord Require: A Guide for Preaching and Teaching Biblical Ethics*. Grand Rapids, MI: Baker Academic, 2009.

Kunhiyop, Samuel Waje. *African Christian Ethics*. Burkura, Nigeria: Word Alive/Hippo, 2008.

Long, D. Stephen. *Christian Ethics: A Very Short Introduction*. New York: Oxford University Press, 2010.

Longenecker, Richard N. *New Testament Social Ethics for Today*. Grand Rapids, MI: Eerdmans, 1984.

MacIntyre, Alasdair. *After Virtue: A Study in Moral Theory*. 3rd ed. Notre Dame, IN: University of Notre Dame Press, 2007.

Mott, Stephen Charles. *Biblical Ethics and Social Change*. New York: Oxford University Press, 1982.

Nullens, Patrick, and Ronald T. Michener. *The Matrix of Christian Ethics: Integrating Philosophy and Moral Theology in a Postmodern Context.* Colorado Springs, CO: Paternoster, 2010.

O'Donovan, Oliver. *Resurrection and Moral Order: An Outline for Evangelical Ethics.* 2nd ed. Grand Rapids, MI: Eerdmans, 1986.

Rae, Scott B. *Moral Choices: An Introduction to Ethics.* 2nd ed. Grand Rapids, MI: Zondervan, 1995, 2000.

Stott, John. *Being a Responsible Christian in a Non-Christian Society.* Vol. 1 of *Involvement.* Old Tappan, NJ: Revell, 1973.

_____. *Decisive Issues Facing Christians Today.* Old Tappan, NJ: Revell, 1984.

_____. *Social and Sexual Relationships in the Modern World.* Vol. 2 of *Involvement.* Old Tappan, NJ: Revell, 1973.

Wells, Samuel, ed. *Christian Ethics: An Introductory Reader.* Malden, MA: Wiley-Blackwell, 2010.

Wells, Samuel, and Ben Quash. *Introducing Christian Ethics.* Malden, MA: Wiley-Blackwell, 2010.

Wogaman, J. Phillip, and Douglas M. Strong. *Readings in Christian Ethics: A Historical Sourcebook.* Louisville: Westminster, 1996.

Wright, N. T. *After You Believe: Why Christian Character Matters.* New York: Harper-One, 2010.

GENERAL INDEX

SCRIPTURE INDEX

✚ CHECK OUT THE OTHER BOOKS IN THE
RECLAIMING THE CHRISTIAN INTELLECTUAL TRADITION SERIES

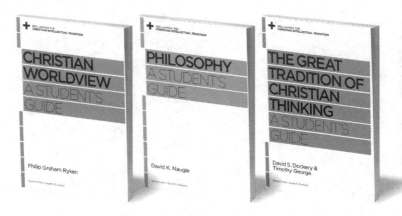

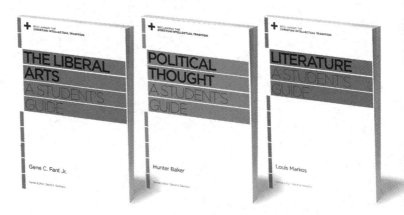

For more information, visit crossway.org.